The Man in Nagasaki

Memories and Other Recollections

by
Jerome D. Oremland, M.D.

Drawings by Benjamin Pierce

Order this book online at www.trafford.com
or email orders@trafford.com

Most Trafford titles are also available at major online book retailers.

© Copyright 2009 Jerome D. Oremland, M. D.
Illustrated by Benjamin Pierce

Note for Librarians: A cataloguing record for this book is available from Library
and Archives Canada at www.collectionscanada.ca/amicus/index-e.html

Printed in Victoria, BC, Canada.

ISBN: 978-1-4251-8729-3

*Our mission is to efficiently provide the world's finest, most comprehensive
book publishing service, enabling every author to experience success.
To find out how to publish your book, your way, and have it available
worldwide, visit us online at www.trafford.com*

Trafford rev. 8/20/2009

Trafford
PUBLISHING®   www.trafford.com

North America & international
toll-free: 1 888 232 4444 (USA & Canada)
phone: 250 383 6864 ♦ fax: 812 355 4082

Dedication and Acknowledgements

The book is dedicated to my wife, Evie, who appears in many of the middle chapters and in many ways in the concluding chapters.

Others who played a pivotal part in bringing these thoughts to print were my son, Noah, who carefully read each passage and helpfully and only somewhat successfully controlled my tendency toward hyperbole and excessive sentimentalism. Noah fortunately rescued quite a few dangling participles. My daughter, Cici Teter, was the ever-careful editor, making sense out of many circuitous passages, clarifying the punctuation, and helping achieve purity in the language.

Great appreciation goes to Benjamin Pierce who added enormously by making visible through his magical pen the poignancy and the humor in the incidents.

Of course, I appreciate my cover endorsers who not only provided succinct statements about the book, but through their comments emboldened me in pursuing the project.

Christine Walsh-Newton deserves many thanks for patiently making the manuscript ready for the computer and providing many helpful and artistic suggestions and Amy Clay of Trafford Press for continuing interest in the project.

Yet, the main players in these memories remain unknown and cannot be acknowledged other than by honoring them with my undying memory of them.

JDO

The Man in Nagasaki
Memories and Other Recollections

Foreword

This book is a record of poignant experiences. Largely they are memories with all the distortions of half-forgotten events. Many are reminiscences, half-visual, half-thought vivid revisitations of adventures. All I hold in memory with special tenderness.

They are essentially stories from my life. I am astonished that they span over 60 years of living. Some come from my adolescence in Wyoming, which only in recent years have I recognized as having given me a sense of self-reliance and the ability to tolerate aloneness. Wyoming's aridness also may have given me an unquenchable thirst for things of beauty and luxuriance. A few of the anecdotes relate to my professional life and the great enrichment it has brought. Some of the stories come during my married and family years; years ended too early and sadly by the death of my dear wife, Evelyn, known in these pages as Evie. It is the cruelest irony that someone known for her loving, nourishing qualities should have the very symbol of those qualities, the breast, turn against her and destroy her. Some of the episodes are from late in my life, as I have had to learn again to live alone, something that comes more easily than it should.

Although throughout I am the protagonist, actually they are less stories about me than about another or about a circumstance. With unusual frequency the "another" is a nameless person, who in ways that I could never have expected, came into my life but briefly and disappeared as quickly, but who then and now changed me.

I hope the reader will keep in mind that these experiences were selected for their interest and often their poignancy, sometimes for their humor. My many unhappy and unsatisfying memories-- even today, the thought of some makes me wince--I have spared both of us.

The Western

(1943)

I was born in the Great Divide Basin that crosses
southwestern Wyoming, one of the most arid parts of North America.
The importance of water and its absence was marked by the names of
the localities. We lived in Rock Springs. Green River was 15 miles
west; Bitter Creek (in Wyoming *creek* rhymes with *crick*) was 30 miles
east; and the county was Sweetwater.

To the north were huge cattle ranches that we called
"spreads," vast homesteads owned by friends of my parents. It is hard
to conceive of the isolation of these ranches. They were connected
to the outside world by rutted dirt roads that were closed most of the
year because of deep snow when they could only be traversed by horse
or by horse-drawn sleigh. These slender and fragile connections led
to the main road, a two-lane asphalt road, itself frequently closed with
snow that ran north from Rock Springs to Yellowstone National Park.

Then, as now, there was always much work to do on a ranch.
There was the endless repair of the fences, the banks of the creeks, the
home, and the various barns and out-buildings. All had to be done

before the deep snows that began in September. The ranches were largely self-sufficient, run by an individual family and two or three regular "hands," as cowboys actually were called.

During spring round-up when the cattle were taken to higher levels, fall round-up when the cattle were returned to the lower reaches of the ranches, and the fall haying when the hay was mowed and stacked for winter feed, the ranchers might take on as many as ten to fifteen extra hands. My family would often visit during these busy times to help their friends.

Even though it was the early 1940s, Wyoming ranches, in fact all of Wyoming, remained entrenched in the 1890s. There was no electricity on the ranches; water was pumped by hand and hauled in pails; the cows were milked twice a day; butter was churned; bread was baked; eggs were gathered; and small vegetables were gardened. All the meat was raised and butchered on the property. Elk, antelope, and wild ducks were shot for food, not for sport, and there was no fish except for fresh caught trout. At night, light was provided by the flickering light of kerosene wick lamps and the ever-present hissing Coleman lantern. Little happened after sunset. All work began at dawn.

When I was very young, I helped in the kitchen. I have lasting memories of one ranch on which my mother and Tiny Noble, the 5' 11" wife of the owner, cooked breakfast daily for the hands. The wood-burning stove was covered with sizzling eggs, huge hot cakes, mounds of bacon, baking biscuits, giant pots of coffee, and a large kettle of thick white gravy (a mixture of milk, flour, salt, and bacon drippings) that was poured over everything.

When I was about 14 years old, I was hired as a summer hand. I herded cattle and cut and stacked hay. It was always great fun to jump into the haystacks. At night, I slept with the other hands in the bunk house, a dank and dreary log cabin with a line of cots. It was then that I learned the truth about cowboys.

Cowboys have no names, only nick names. They were Red, Slim, Tex, Shorty, Sandy, Dutch, Duke, and Bud. Sometimes there was a Nick or a Tom. No one knew where they came from; no one knew where they were going; and no one asked. They just appeared during the hiring seasons, asking for work. If they seemed right to the owner, they were hired on the spot. At times the owner recognized them from previous seasons, but largely the hands just came and went.

The cowboys owned nothing. They usually had a small satchel with cards, a cribbage board, Western magazines, and sparse personal articles. Their prized possession was their boots. They actually slept with their boots on for fear they might be stolen. At night they lay on the bunks reading their Westerns or playing a solitary kind of cribbage. It is only in the myth of the West and in Hollywood that cowboys have a devoted horse and sing around a campfire.

Always cordial, the hands said little. When they did talk, they always looked at their boots. They only looked you straight in the eye when they were angry. They spoke with exaggerated politeness and an almost gothic formality. When talking with a woman, they would follow most sentences with "ma'am" and with the owner, "sir." They usually called me "Kid" as in "Hey, kid. Do you want . . . ?"

As an aside, it was not until years later when I worked in the hospital in Jackson Hole, Wyoming, and cowboys came in injured from the rodeo or ranches that I learned who some of them were. Most came from the East, although some came from California. It was a great surprise to learn that some came from well-to-do families. I know of two circumstances in which these solitary men owned the ranches on which they worked. These two ranches, run by managers, had been bought by rich Eastern families for their loner, often black sheep, sons. I am not sure that the young men knew that they owned the ranches. As I progressed in my psychiatric training, I realized that many of these cowboys were simple schizophrenics who adopted a Western tradition. They were essentially drifters fearful of any relationship and of any responsibility.

The hands and the ranchers worked extremely hard, side by side, from daybreak to dark, all week. Saturday was pay day, and Saturday night the hands would drive to the nearest town, see a movie--a Western, of course--get drunk, spend all their money, get into a brawl, be piled into the back of a pick-up truck by a buddy, driven back to the ranch, and dumped onto their bunks. Sunday was spent in great remorse with giant hangovers and silent promises "never to do that again," only to repeat the drama the following weekend.

One summer I was lucky enough to get work on a ranch near Jackson in the Jackson Hole valley of Wyoming. Although it was the main town in Jackson Hole, it was only a minor tourist attraction near the Teton Range and generally a place for a brief stop on the way to Yellowstone National Park. Jackson then was a very different place from what it is today. The economy of the Jackson Hole relied largely on ranching. The dude ranch and sport hunting and fishing were in their infancy, and skiing was only for the most experienced and adventurous.

Jackson had a movie theater called The Teton Theater (in Wyoming, *theater* rhymes with *alligator*). A few near-by small towns also had movie houses, as they were called, but Jackson's had a tremendous advantage. It had two projectors, which meant that the films were shown in continuous format. The other movie houses had to interrupt the show after each reel for rewinding before the next reel could be shown.

I managed to get a second job running the projectors at The Teton on Friday and Saturday nights. The projectors were in a small closed room behind and above the last row of seats. The projection room had two small window openings that faced the screen, each with a projector mounted behind it. Each projector was lighted by a carbon arc. These arcs were essentially two carbon probes separated by a gap that had to be carefully adjusted so that the high voltage electricity running between them produced an intense, very white light that passed through the film to project the image onto the screen. The projection room was hot and stuffy, filled with clattering machinery and the hiss and smell of the arcs.

All the movies shown at The Teton were four "reelers" and, of course, were Westerns. They came in two large cans, two to a can. One can on the outside was numbered in red paint #1 and #2; the second can #3 and #4. Before the showing, I would splice in the previews, the *Movietone News,* and the cartoon before the first reel.

After the theater was darkened, the arc was lighted in projector #1, and reel #1 would begin to run. At the proper moment, the diaphragm in front of the arc was lifted, and the image would magically appear on the screen.

Always the preview was met with tremendous hooting and yelling of angry complaints. The audience was impatient for the feature to begin. The uproar over the previews was mild compared to the greeting given the *Movietone News*. However, the cartoon always brought loud cheers.

These fellows (rarely were any women in the theater) invented the interactive audience. They would shout, stamp their feet, and jump up in their chairs as they became fully absorbed in the action of the movie. During any chase scene the theater was filled with men jumping in their seats yelling "Get 'em! Get 'em!" When they approved of the action, there were hoots and hollers. Disapproval brought loud booing and a variety of uncouth noises. Their language was never foul; in fact there was a taboo against what they called "cussing." The noises were closer to animal sounds, a variety of hoots and howls.

After reel #1 was well underway, projector #2 was made ready and reel #2 would be threaded and the carbon arc of projector #2 lighted. The films were (and still are) marked so that the projectionist by watching the screen can switch smoothly from projector #1 to projector #2. As the movie played, in the upper right-hand corner of the screen a brief white flash appeared as the signal to have the arc ready and begin running the film in projector #2. A second brief white flash indicated that the projectionist must lower the diaphragm of projector #1 and simultaneously lift the diaphragm of projector #2. This process was repeated for reel #3 and reel #4, in sequence.

If the projectionist were not skillful and had not properly timed the sequencing, a series of black numbers would appear on a white background before the picture again resumed. With practice I became quite skillful in coordinating the projectors. In effect, I had to be skillful, because ineptness, although rare, was little tolerated by The Teton's very critical audience.

When all went well, at the movie's end, the crowd tumbled out of the movie house to go to the local bars, which inevitably ended in the drunken brawls and a miserable trip back to the ranch in the back of a pick-up truck, as mentioned, the ritual prelude to Sunday's lament.

One Saturday night after I had completed running reel #1 and projector #2 was noisily projecting, I opened the second can to take out reel #3 when, to my horror, I noted that it was marked reel #2. I quickly looked at reel #4, which was properly marked. I realized that following reel #1, I was now showing reel #3. Reel #2 was sitting in the second can next to reel #4.

I panicked. Clearly, there was no possibility of explaining or apologizing. All I could do was to follow reel #3 with reel #2 and then to follow reel #2 with reel #4. Of course that meant that the sweet young woman who came from the East was already in the West before she arrived from the East; that the older woman with a heart of gold helped the hero out of his mess before he had gotten into it; and that the bad guys were driven out of town before they had arrived.

Knowing my audience, I locked the door to the projection room fearing a riot. The movie ended. To my profound relief, there was only happy hooting and cheering as the audience exited.

Clearly the cowboys of the Old West lived in a mythical world. Each lived his version of the "Western," and week after week, each went to the movies not to see the movie but to reaffirm an invisible world of his own making.

The End of the Old West

(1951)

While I was in medical school at Stanford University, I returned home to Wyoming during my summers to work as an extern at the hospital in Jackson. Jackson had one small hospital, actually a two-story log cabin, with a few nurses. In the town were two doctors, both general practitioners, whose offices were in their homes not far from the hospital. Because the hospital census increased during the summer, it was decided to hire a medical student, an extern, to help admit patients, keep track of patient records, and help the doctors and nurses with patient care. I was the first extern hired.

I slept on the second floor of the log cabin in a small room and enjoyed being called doctor, although most knew that I was a medical student. In the hospital, I wore a white coat over blue jeans. To the delight of the "Eastern folk," the doctors often showed up in jeans, cowboy boots, and a cowboy hat.

At night I was alone in the hospital with the on-duty nurse. Frequently I would be called to check a patient who had had surgery, often a child who had had a tonsillectomy. I provided emergency triage to anyone who came directly to the emergency room of the hospital until a doctor could arrive. At night there was also the rare child with a high fever. Mostly there were many ranching accidents and some terrible car accidents, usually when a car hit a wild animal on the open road.

Occasionally, one of the doctors would arrive on horseback with a second already saddled horse. He would call up to my window and yell for me to get some medical equipment. Together we would ride into the hills to tend a serious problem in an isolated cabin.

On Saturday afternoons I provided the medical coverage for the local rodeo. I would sit in a pick-up truck and wait next to the ring. At the crunching sound of cracked bones, I would drive into the arena, examine the injured man, and if necessary load him into the back of the pick-up truck to take him to the hospital.

In short it was a wonderful experience in a beautiful place working with wonderful people. I felt blessed. I was in a situation where I could learn a great deal, and I had great responsibility.

One night, the nurse on duty called me rather anxiously. "Someone has been shot," she cried out. I ran downstairs to the emergency room. On the examining table was a young cowboy. By his side was an older man whom I recognized as "an owner," that is, a rancher.

I could see that the young man had been shot in the chest and instituted the proper emergency measures. Soon a town doctor arrived. He congratulated me on what I had done, and he assured the patient and the owner that the man would recover. He then left.

I asked the waiting rancher what had happened. In the dry, laconic manner that characterized the men of Wyoming, he said, "Well, Jim here was messing around with the cook. I told him to lay off her, and he didn't follow my advice. When she complained again, I fired him. He packed his gear and left. That was a couple of days ago. This evening, when I was driving back to the ranch, he jumped down from a rock onto the back of my truck. I think he's been seeing too many cowboy movies, and he aimed a rifle at me. I grabbed my gun and shot him and brought him here."

I said, "You better go to the sheriff and tell him." He answered, "I already done that." There was not much more to be said. Justice in Wyoming at the time was a rather pragmatic affair.

About three days later when the cowboy was almost fully recovered, I was dressing his wound when he looked at me and said, "Doc, you know it was my boss who shot me." I said, "I know." He then looked down at his boots the way cowboys do when they are about to ask for something. There was a long pause. He drawled, "Do you think 'cause it was my boss who shot me, I am entitled to workman's compensation?"

I felt I had just witnessed the end of the Old West.

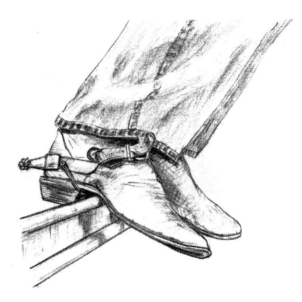

A Lost Soul in Japan

(1953)

The year was 1953 and as a young lieutenant, junior grade, in

the U.S. Navy, I was assigned to the *USS Prairie*, AD-15, a destroyer

tender. The *Prairie*, over 530 feet long and 74 feet beam, was

commissioned in 1940. With its complement of nearly 1,700 men,

the *Prairie* contained extensive carpenter, machine, and electrical

repair shops of all kinds. It was a source of great pride that the *Prairie*

could perform almost any kind of repair a destroyer might need.

The ship had a full sick bay, an operating room, two doctors, five

hospital corps men, and a complete dental service with six dentists

and eight technicians. Equipped with cannons fore and aft and side

gunnery, the *Prairie* was also a warship and completely sea worthy. It

occasionally traveled to other Asian ports where destroyers gathered

for repairs, but its primary mission was to rotate between San Diego,

California, and Sasebo, Japan.

I joined the *Prairie* while it was in Hawaii on its way to

Sasebo. Officially I was part of the Flag--that is, I was assigned to

the admiral and his staff who oversaw several divisions of destroyers in Asia. Although I had medical duties on the ship, my main responsibilities were with the Flag as part of the admiral's staff. This gave me almost complete freedom. Because the *Prairie* had the Flag aboard, when in port we always had a prime berth on the most convenient pier, allowing for easy coming and going. I shared a stateroom with another doctor, and I was very comfortable. In short, I had a sweet deal.

While in Sasebo, one day I was called by the admiral. "Come on in, Jerry," he said without looking up. He rarely called me "Jerry." When he did, it meant that he had a task that was outside my official duties. He continued, "There is a young ensign AWOL." Because we were technically at war, AWOL was a serious matter, but I knew that the charge carried a considerable level of elasticity.

"How can I help, sir?" I responded. The admiral went on, "His name is Jason. He is only 22, a recent graduate of the Academy, and a line officer. His buddies say he received a 'Dear John' letter from his girlfriend. They mentioned that he was 'straight-arrow.' Do you want to see if you can find him? You can use my car and driver." In the U.S. Navy there was no such thing as a request from an admiral. I responded with a smart, "Aye, aye, Sir." I did add, "You know, Sir, I am a doctor and not an M.P. (Military Police)." He caught the drift of my response and said, "If he comes back with you, we will treat it as a medical and not a legal matter."

The port of Sasebo sits on the southern island of Kyushu. Because of its large and deep harbor, it was formerly a large Japanese naval base. During the United States occupation of Japan, it became an important U.S. Navy base with docks and moorings for many large naval vessels.

The base was surrounded by an imposing fence, within which were temporary buildings to support operations, a movie theater, the Officers' Club, the Non-Commissioned Officers' Club, and the Enlistment Men's Club. All of the clubs served American-style food. Hamburgers were especially popular. The club bars also served extremely inexpensive drinks. The 10-cent martinis were a favorite at the Officers' Club, but the N.C.O. Club only served beer, and no alcoholic beverages were sold at the E.M. Club. There was a strict unspoken code that there was no socialization on or off duty among the three tiers.

"Indigenous people," that is, Japanese people, were not allowed on the base socially, so there were no women in the Officers' Club, the N.C.O. Club, or the E.M. Club, except for the few nurses who were commissioned officers and therefore allowed in the Officers' Club. The Navy was segregated, so there were no black officers or enlisted men except for the officers' stewards who had a society all of their own. A Navy base in those days was essentially a white male fraternity divided into three horizontal societies. However, as a doctor, I enjoyed a special and peculiar place in the hierarchy. In that I dealt directly with and knew the intimate details about both the enlisted men and the officers, I traveled easily among the strict segregation that characterized military life.

When off duty and on leaving the ship, there was little for anyone to do other than go to the base movies, which were largely re-runs, participate in sports team activities, drink at the base clubs, or go into town. Mostly the officers and enlisted men alike went to the town to dance, drink, and find a girl for the night.

The town was a rabbit warren of small, old, pre-war buildings and shack-like houses. The narrow streets quickly ascended into hills. Most of the shacks were bars, "establishments" as they were called, all of which had "hostesses" who stood on the street to entice the sailors for drinking, dancing, and sex.

The bars were carefully marked N.C.O or E.M., meaning that they were limited to noncommissioned officers or enlisted men. Higher on the hill was the famous (in its day) Matsu Lodge, an establishment limited to commissioned officers. The Lodge was a well run, rather attractive, larger establishment that overlooked the harbor. It had a large dance floor, several bars, hostesses, and of course, many small rooms.

Some of the officers and men quickly formed alliances with Japanese women and rented "homes" where they "lived" with their "girlfriends." Many in the regular Navy, who rotated to Japan every 6 months, essentially carried out two lives. They had their families in San Diego and their girlfriends in Sasebo, keeping both year around. There was an unspoken rule that what happened in "the field" stayed in "the field."

As a doctor, I well knew the full extent of the sexual activities of the sailors. In addition to treating the men, I would visit the houses where the men had been infected and treat the girls to decrease possible further infections. My visits were very welcome, and great occasion was made over *O-ishi-san* (the honorable physician). While I was there, I was asked to treat other minor problems--sore throats, colds, headaches, infected toes, and the like. In a short period of time, I knew most of the *mama-sans* and many of the prostitutes in Sasebo.

The *mama-sans* knew the servicemen and loved to joke with and tease them, as well as me. They carefully watched over their establishments, and rough behavior was severely punished. An abusive man was immediately ejected from the house and forbidden to return. There was silent and instant communication among the *mama-sans.* If a man were repeatedly abusive, he was denied access to any house. Sometimes these ejections and refusals were reinforced by a few thug-type Japanese men to whom the *mama-sans* had access.

A quiet drunk, of course, was tolerated and even nursed back to health. The *mama-sans* made sure that the men, no matter how drunk, who had to return to their ships by a particular time were sent on their way. Much of the *mama-sans'* concern was fear of trouble with the Military Police for running an unruly house, but much was also genuine affection for these young men, really boys, whom they knew were far from home and lonely.

The girls in the establishments were very young, giggly, and fun loving. Most were simple girls from the countryside whose fathers had been killed in the war and whose families could not care for them. They loved jokes, games, and especially American music and American dancing. Many had the vain hope of becoming a "war bride" and being taken to the United States or at least becoming a "girlfriend" in a "home." In fact, fraternization was prohibited, and although there were a few marriages, it required a long, technical battle with the sailor's fighting many levels of administrative obstruction.

From Jason's fellow young officers, I learned that, indeed, he was "straight-arrow." They told me that he always stayed close to the ship, the base, and his buddies. He was religious, was devoted to his girlfriend, whom he talked about marrying, never drank to excess, and did not participate in the widely available prostitution that characterized the military life overseas of those days. Although I did not know Jason, I knew other young officers like him. They carried many unacknowledged fears about the strangeness of Japan, its food, its customs, and its people. They stayed close to the ship and the base. They covered their fear by inhibition that was often rationalized as being "loyal to the girl back home." This rationalization often quickly broke down.

Talking to the hospital corpsmen on the ship confirmed that they could never remember Jason's having lined up for condoms or penicillin pills (a protection against venereal disease used at that time) before going on leave in Sasebo. I knew that he had never been treated for gonorrhea, "clap" in Navy language, because although the enlisted men stood in long lines three days after each weekend ashore (the incubation period of gonorrhea), the officers had the special privilege of consulting privately with a doctor, namely me.

After talking with Jason's friends and confirming the admiral's suspicions regarding the "Dear John" letter, it seemed clear that Jason had to be hiding in Sasebo, most likely in a brothel.

I first went to the Matsu Lodge and asked the *mama-san,*

whom I knew very well, if Jason had been there. Her first question was, "Is he in trouble?" I explained, "Not if I can find him and take him back." Her response, "Do I have your word?"

"Yes," I said, explaining that I had cleared it with the admiral that if I brought him back there would be no legal action. By her questions, I knew that he had been there.

She explained, "He was here two nights ago and very drunk. I tried to get him to go back to the ship, but he refused. He left in the middle of the night. He left these." She brought out a small lacquer box. In it meticulously folded were his cap, uniform, and shoes. I noticed that his skivvies (T-shirt and shorts) and socks had been carefully washed, ironed, and folded.

I reasoned that by ridding himself of his uniform, he must be traveling in wooden clogs and a *yukata,* the short cotton kimono that visitors are given to wear when they arrive in Japanese inns and establishments. I surmised that Jason must be headed for one of the hundreds of tiny enlisted men's brothels where without his officer's uniform he could hide.

I asked the *mama-san* if she knew where he had gone. Her reply, "I have no idea," was accompanied by the name of a certain *mama-san.* It was her way of telling me where to go next. I told my driver, an enlisted man, who recognized the name of the *mama-san* and knew the brothel. Quickly we arrived and I received the usual honorific greeting, invitation to tea, and a good deal of teasing from the girls. I asked the *mama-san* the same questions and received the same query, "Is he in trouble?" I gave the same reply, and she whispered something to my driver. Off we went.

At the next place, as we drove up we were greeted by the *mama-san.* Word obviously was preceding us. Without asking, she volunteered that he had been there, was very drunk, and had left. She said she did not know where he went, but she whispered something to the driver, who obviously was a frequent visitor to her establishment.

On my fourth try, the *mama-san* was very hesitant. She asked several times if Jason were in trouble. Repeatedly I assured her, "Not if can take him back to the ship." Several times she implored, "Do you promise?" I replied, "I am a doctor, not an M.P." She then led me to a small shack behind her establishment. There was Jason in a deep drunken sleep. I noted that he was recently shaven and in a clean *yukata*. Next to him was a girl who obviously had been taking care of him.

I shook him. Dimly he rose to semi-consciousness and recognized me. I talked about the letter and told him that if he came with me, I would admit him to the sick bay. I told him I had the admiral's promise that there would be no legal action--that at the most he would receive a three-day leave of absence without pay. He staggered to his feet, and we thanked the girl and the *mama-san*. The driver and I helped Jason stumble into the car.

We were on our way down the hill toward the harbor when I heard, *"O-ishi-san, O-ishi-san!"* I looked back and saw the *mama-san* running down the hill, her kimono flapping, and her wooden clogs clattering on the cobblestones. We stopped the car, and she handed me a small lacquer box. In it were Jason's dog tags, watch, ring, and wallet. "He forgot these," she said.

Three days later, sober and returned to duty, Jason came to the sick bay and sheepishly asked me to treat him for the clap.

It is questionable whether Jason learned something about Japan, but without question I did. I will always remember how caring and protective the young girls and old women were of this sad young man, a member of an armed force once the agent in their destruction. I have to add that often when my faith in humankind falters, I see that elderly woman, kimono flying and clogs chattering, running down the hill to return Jason's valuables. It has become a reassurance of my faith in the goodness of at least some, perhaps most, people.

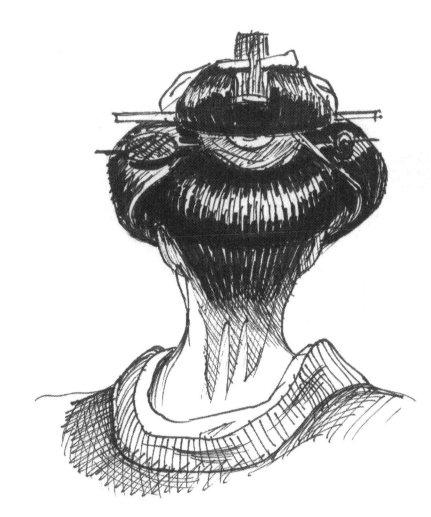

Sasebo

(1953)

The port of Sasebo resides on the southern island of Kyushu where Japan peters out into a series of wooded, rocky islands, extending south to Okinawa and beyond. Although I was there nearly a year, my memories of Sasebo are limited. I think that is because Sasebo was limited. Yet I have a vivid memory of a Japanese fisherman. As is often the case in the memories that comprise this book, he remains unnamed even though he was responsible for introducing me to the aesthetics of Japan. In fact, it was he who raised in me an aesthetic appreciation that I did not know I had.

I do not remember how I met him, but I think I was walking along the old port and I spotted a tiny boat at a dock. I asked a few people about the boat and eventually found its owner, an old fisherman. I think of him as old, but actually I have no idea of his age. His skin was coarsely weathered, and he had only a few terrible teeth. But, there was aliveness in his eyes. He walked with a marked limp that he skillfully tried to conceal. It was clear that he, as all the Japanese at that time, had known the war in some personal way.

He spoke no English. With the help of a boy and a lot of sign language I learned that he often used the boat for fishing for his family and friends. I had long yearned to explore the tiny islands that extended south from Sasebo into the East China Sea. I told him I had no interest in fishing but that I would like to boat around in the islands and perhaps swim. He understood, and before long, often on a Sunday I would meet him and off we would go.

The islands were incredibly close together, rocky outcroppings with numerous pines growing in the crags. The water surrounding them was very deep, beautifully warm, crystal clear, and mirrored the islands and their tufts of green. There was a large tidal shift, but no surf, and I could dive from the rocks into the deep water, often swimming from island to island. The fisherman seemed to know the best places for me to disembark. Later, at a prearranged time, I could hear his puffing engine and I knew that his ancient vessel was on its way to retrieve me. Silently we would return to the port as the sun set on scenes of exotic beauty.

I well remember one evening when he picked me up. Very hesitantly he addressed me, *"O-ishi-san, O-ishi-san!"* In his pidgin English, I could make out that he was asking if I wanted to see something special. I was curious, and he could not explain.

On returning to the harbor, he motioned for me to follow

him. We went to his not-too-trusty-looking and very rusty motorbike. He mounted, and then I mounted on the back. The poor machine struggled as it carried the two of us up into the hills behind Sasebo. At a point the man stopped and indicated where I should sit. Before long a small group of Japanese gathered. I was completely mystified. My friend pointed to signify "Look!"

The full moon had reached a perfect point in relation to a snarled tree on a not very distant hill. The tree, the moon, the hill, and the gathering mist below developed an artist perfection never to be forgotten. As the moon passed, the small crowd dispersed as silently as it had assembled.

The Man in Nagasaki

(1954)

Although World War II had been over for 9 years, the United States occupation of Japan continued. As a young U.S. Navy doctor, I was part of that occupation. We, the victorious Americans, easily maintained a defensive arrogance and superiority. Largely we were inured to the great destruction that had befallen those tiny, heavily populated islands, although it is true that by 1954 most of the rubble from the war had been cleared. In fact, the attitude was that the Japanese had brought this on themselves and that they deserved what their war-like expansionist attitudes had reaped. For us, Japan was largely a country of women--old women controlling young women in taxi dance halls, bars, and whore houses. It was unspoken, yet clear, that most of the Japanese men had been killed during the long years of war.

Early on I suspected that there was something beyond the officers' clubs and the dance halls with women paid for company. For reasons not clear, I felt compelled to seek out Japan. In looking back, I am proud of that young, if naïve, adventurous spirit that resided deeply inside of me.

It was in the spirit of trying to find Japan, combined with a morbid curiosity about the atom bomb, that in late fall 1954 I set out for Nagasaki. Little did I expect that the trip would stay with me for the rest of my life.

Of course the only way I could travel was by train. As required, I traveled in uniform and carried only a small duffle, camera, and topcoat. I had no difficulty navigating the then rather simple rail system and easily found a seat. I was used to traveling with my knees jammed onto the back of the seat in front of me. At 6 feet tall, everything in Japan was small. I towered over the people and was constantly bumping into things. Entering any building required ducking.

My excitement mounted when the conductor bowed on entering the car and called out, "Nagasaki." Yet as I hopped off the train onto the platform, I became somewhat hesitant. I had no guide books or maps. As I looked for a sign indicating the way to the station, I was approached by a man, probably in his late thirties, dressed in rather worn western clothes. Bowing deeply, in careful English the man asked, "Are you American?" Hesitantly I answered, "Yes." He continued, "Would you like me to show you Nagasaki?"

I was leery, but agreed. The man offered to carry my bag and coat, and with hesitation I followed him into the street. It never occurred to me to ask his name.

The man hailed a rickshaw, and as we climbed into the back he spoke in Japanese to the boy. We were off. The rickshaws of the 1950s were small motorcycles with an attached two-wheeled seat that could be covered in the rain. On the poorly repaired streets, the ride was indeed bumpy, but this did not keep the rickshaw boys from careening around the corners. Being young, I gave it no thought and enjoyed the thrill.

We drove into a markedly desolate area, and the rickshaw labored up a small mound to a bombed-out, obviously western-style brick structure with remnants of gothic tracery. The man paid for the rickshaw ride. I wondered when the reckoning would come.

The man said, "This was the Catholic cathedral. It was at the center of the bomb blast." With morbid curiosity, I explored the windowless few walls that formed a corner. Nothing else remained. From that knoll with the remnants of the cathedral behind me, I looked over a wasteland. The barrenness, divided by a river with treeless banks, was interrupted only by vague outlines of foundations.

My youthful curiosity developed a twinge of guilt and even more of fear. I suddenly realized I was at the epicenter of the atom bomb explosion.

The man said that after the explosion the dead were brought to the river bed and the river was filled with bodies. Even though I had wanted to see the site of the atom bomb destruction, long-held thoughts that the bomb had shortened the war and saved thousands of lives proved not sustaining. I just wanted to get out of there.

To my relief, the man said, "We go to Butterfly House. It is beautiful." In another rickshaw, we traveled to what must have been the other side of the city, a beautiful, if somewhat ragged area. We climbed a hill and came to a garden with a large Victorian house that was intact but shabby. I remember the huge veranda that encircled the house with its commanding view of the beautiful harbor, somewhat rebuilt and very active with various tugs, barges, and ships. As we walked around the veranda, laughingly the man said, "Of course there was no Madam Butterfly, only many Madam Butterflies. Before the war, this house was a tourist site. We called it 'The Butterfly House' because it was the home of a Scottish man and his Japanese wife."

At the garden's edge, I spied a couple. The young man was dressed in shabby western clothes, and the young woman wore a beautiful, I even remember, red kimono with a heavily embroidered yellow and gold *obi* and *geta* (the traditional Japanese wooden sandal). I wanted to take her picture and motioned to the man to

36

stand aside so that I could have a picture of *"Chio Chio-san."* When I finished, the man motioned to me that I should stand next to the woman so that he could take a picture of "You, Pinkerton!" Suddenly I was aware of an erosion of Western arrogance. I was the visitor and an object to be viewed. Even today, it amuses me to think that somewhere in Japan on some mantle or in some scrapbook is a picture of the beautiful young woman in her red kimono and me in my U.S. Navy uniform.

The man and I continued to explore the garden, walking for the most part in silence. Our lack of conversation was only partly due to language difficulties. Mostly it was because the man was consistently diffident. Yet something did develop between us. I think he sensed that I, although naïve, wanted to learn about Japan and appreciated what I was seeing.

As the sun lowered in the autumn afternoon, the man asked if I had ever been to a tea house. "No," I said, and we walked briskly to a small establishment on a river bank. It was set in a bamboo forest and was quite isolated. I had been in Japan long enough to know Japanese customs and handily removed my shoes. Even though in those days I could easily sit on the floor, I never mastered sitting in the Japanese style, resting on my heels and with my back erect. Generally, I sat cross-legged.

An older woman in a kimono carefully prepared lukewarm, frothy green tea and served some small rice cakes. The tea tasted swampy to me, and the cakes were nearly tasteless. Nonetheless, I was excited to think that I was finding Japan. The man paid for the refreshments and amid much bowing we left to continue walking.

Evening neared, and he asked, "Have you ever been to a geisha house?" Suddenly my suspicions were confirmed. I thought, "Here's the pitch. He's a pimp." I said that I wasn't sure what he had in mind. He repeated, "You go to geisha house?" I was very aware of the extent of prostitution in Japan, especially in the port cities where the bars with taxi dance girls and whore houses, separately and combined, were the main entertainment for the U.S. sailors. Not sure into what I was getting but intrigued by the proposal, I approached the idea cautiously. Recognizing my hesitation, the man said, "No, no. Not girl. Geisha." My curiosity overcame my trepidations, and again we were off in a rickshaw careening into the Nagasaki night.

We traveled some distance. I must confess that all the time I was in Nagasaki I had no idea of where I was. We crossed a small river and were let off in front of a low, arched bridge that crossed over a canal to the front of a house. The house was a traditional, two-story, wooden Japanese house. I remember thinking how charming it was with the light coming through the *shoji* screen and the lighted, single large paper lantern outside. In the entrance garden, I was greeted by a young woman in kimono. The man stayed outside with my duffle, coat, and camera.

I entered and obeying custom removed my shoes. Together, the young woman and I moved silently over the wooden hallway floor. We came to a room, and she fell to her knees. Sliding open doors, she revealed a large *tatami* room. One side opened onto a small garden, and in the corner was the *tokonoma* (a traditional niche common in tatami rooms) with a hanging scroll and a small flower arrangement of yellow and white chrysanthemums. I entered. She handed me the *yukata*, the highly starched, lightweight, blue and white cotton kimono that one wears in Japanese establishments be they whore houses or *ryokans* (inns).

I quickly realized that this place was different from the whore houses of Sasebo in that the woman turned away while I undressed. Once I was in my yukata, she said something about the *ofuro* (the bath) and led me to a small room with a sunken wooden tub filled with hot water. Again, unlike Sasebo, the woman left me while I soaped, washed, and then soaked in the hot water. The young woman returned with a very small towel and coquettishly, but modestly, helped me dry myself.

When we returned to my room, I saw that a low table had been set. The woman began to prepare *shabu-shabu,* beef and vegetables boiled in broth. She carefully placed each cut of meat and the vegetables into the boiling water and poured sake for me. As each morsel was cooked, she placed it on a bowl of rice and ceremoniously handed me the bowl. I am sure the meal had been selected with Western taste in mind.

As I was eating, the door silently slid open, and there was the geisha. Young and slight, she was wearing a magnificent, multicolored kimono and a gold obi embroidered with many cranes in flight. In her elaborately done hair were richly decorated pins from which hung strands of tiny artificial flowers and jewel-like beads. Her face was bone white, and her eyebrows and eyes were heavily accented. Her mouth was a brilliant, tiny rosebud. She walked as though floating. Without effort she sat on her heels, back erect, and spoke some soft words that I could not understand. She had a *shami-sen* (a stringed musical instrument) and began plucking away. Before long the room was filled with a soft song in that strange high-pitched falsetto that characterizes the female Japanese singing voice.

When I had finished eating, the young woman silently removed the utensils, and the geisha came closer and sat beside me. We had no words. From her obi she took out a pencil and a small pad of paper. On it she traced a Tic-Tac-Toe. She smiled sweetly, always lowering her eyes as we played the game with much teasing and laughter. She brought out some string, and we played Cat's Cradle. I was amazed at how much was being communicated without words.

The young woman brought in a small phonograph. The geisha played a Japanese record, and I recognized that she was playing "The Coal Miners' Dance." We began this highly stylized dance that I had learned from encounters with other Japanese women. We circled the room, with my imitating her steps and hand motions. We again sat, and she played the shami-sen and sang.

I thought she said something like "jitterbug," and I realized she was asking me if I could jitterbug, which was all the rage in Japan at the time. She selected a record for the phonograph, and the room was filled with the big band sound of "In the Mood." I realized that she wanted me to teach her to jitterbug. I began teaching her the steps with some difficulty because of the tightness of her kimono. Several times in a sweep of dance drama, one or two of her hair pins fell from her heavily lacquered hair. We laughed as she picked them up, and in a seductive way she asked me to replace them. Next she asked if I could teach her to rumba, and she selected "Besame Mucho." Even in her tight kimono, I sensed a rhythmic body.

It was quite late when she whispered in my ear, "Would you like me to spend the night?" An astonished "Yes" came easily. Without visible signal, the young woman came in with a large, painted folding screen. The geisha and the young woman stepped behind it, and after what seemed like an eternity the geisha emerged in a simple white kimono. Her hair fell like two black crescents that edged her eyes. She had removed her geisha make-up and wig, and she wore only simple powder. She was younger and more beautiful than I had thought. I realized how tiny was her lithe body.

Silently, the young woman placed futons on the floor and covered them with sheets so starched that they barely touched. Looking down and with a deep bow, she left, closing the sliding doors.

The next morning when I awoke, I was alone. After a short time, the door slid open and in came the young woman with a simple Japanese breakfast and a cheerful, *"Ohayo gozaimasu"* (Good morning). She moved a lacquered box toward me, and in it I found my clothes laundered and pressed. I dressed, and when I emerged the young woman led me to the entrance where a very old woman in a pale pink, simple kimono was standing. She bowed deeply and said, *"Domo arigato"* (Thank you). I replied with many "Domo arigato"s.

As I stepped outside into a dewy morning, I suddenly became

aware that I had no idea of where I was or how to get anyplace. I also realized I did not have my duffle, camera, or topcoat. I turned around and there was the man and a rickshaw. He smiled broadly, bowed deeply, and asked, "Did you like geisha?" I could only say *"Hai"* (Yes).

The man said that he must leave. I responded, "I must return to the ship." He replied, "I will take you to the train station."

We arrived at the station shortly before the train arrived and stood about somewhat awkwardly. I was apprehensive, thinking about how much this adventure would cost and how I would pay for it. I thought of my Rolex watch that I had purchased in Hong Kong. Knowing it was something the Japanese prized, I thought, "If worse comes to worse and I do not have enough money, probably it would do as payment."

As the train approached, I said rather stiffly, "How much do I owe you?" He bowed and softly said, "Nothing." He paused and then said, "Every couple of months I come to the station. I find an American service man. I want to show him the beauty of Japan." He looked away. There was a long silence followed by, "It is my penance." There was another long silence, and softly he said, "for what we did to Japan."

I was dumbfounded. Ashamedly, I thought, "And I took him

for a pimp." He handed me my things, bowed deeply, and left. As I stepped onto the train, I realized that I did not know his name; nor he, mine. I did know that I would never forget Japan or him.

*****

Reluctant to confront the changes in Japan and in me, it took 50 years to gather the courage to revisit Japan. In planning a return, I read of a beautiful Japanese restaurant in Kyoto on Pontocho-Dori, a narrow lane lined with old, converted geisha houses along the river Kamo. I called from San Francisco to reserve a Japanese room for dinner. When I told them I would be alone, the voice 6,000 miles away said, "Won't you be lonely?"

When I arrived at the restaurant, the owner greeted me. He was very pleased that someone from as far away as San Francisco had heard of his restaurant. He led me to a beautiful tatami room overlooking the river. I noticed that he left the sliding door separating my room from the adjacent room half open. In the adjacent room were three Japanese women eating. One, much older, her back erect, was wearing a lavender kimono. With her were two young women in beautiful, delicately flowered kimonos. Their faces were perfectly made up. The owner said that he was honored because two *maiko* (apprentice geisha) were celebrating their teacher's retirement.

The owner opened the door wider and the women smiled, beckoning me to enter. The man left saying, "Maybe you won't be so lonely."

The women spoke very little English, but we were able to communicate a little with a lot of laughter and mime before they had to leave. It was not lost on me that the older geisha was about the age that the woman I had met long ago now would be.

It was about midnight when I crossed the bridge over the Kamo and found the old geisha area of Kyoto, the Hanamikoji-dori. On the way, I passed several prostitutes in short, tight pants, long boots, and very tight sweaters with bare navels. They called out, "Where you go, mister? Want some fun?" I thought, "Little changes in Japan."

The Hanamikoji-dori was deserted. There was a light rain, and the tea houses looked like a Hokusai watercolor with the lighted lanterns in front and dim light coming through the shoji. To my delight, I saw a path of light coming out of one of the houses and knew that a door had been opened. Several women in lovely kimonos came out, and amid much bowing, I saw a young geisha leave. She was in full geisha costume. She put up her parasol. Her steps were so graceful that her geta made only a fluttering sound. As she passed, she lowered her eyes, and there was a faint smile.

I returned to my ryokan. As I slid alone between the crisp sheets on the futon, I thought of the man in Nagasaki whom I knew I could never thank. As I stared up at the ceiling, I felt completed--that keeping the memory of the gracious beauty of Japan all these years was thanks enough. I decided that I would not revisit Nagasaki.

The Old Bridge

(1956)

In February 1956, I interrupted my psychiatric training in San Francisco to begin a clerkship (pronounced *clarkship*) in a famous neurological hospital in London, The National Hospital for Nervous Disease at Queens Square, known worldwide as Queens Square. It is hard to remember what England and the Continent were like in 1956. World War II had been over 11 years, yet Europe had barely recovered from the war's ravages. Although largely cleared of rubble, there had been little rebuilding, and everywhere in Europe vast areas of emptiness remained.

I was not disappointed in what I was learning or experiencing at the hospital, but by May, after 4 months of England's cold and dark, I was eager to explore the Continent and to go south to the sun.

I learned that Yugoslavia had just opened to American visitors. The idea of going someplace heretofore forbidden intrigued me. I also hoped that Yugoslavia might be inexpensive.

There was no travel literature available about Yugoslavia, and in fact, little travel information was available about Europe in general. After some searching, in an old bookshop in Bloomsbury near my "digs" I found a small book entitled *A Fortnight in Yugoslavia*. Although printed in the early 1950s, it was filled with incredibly archaic English expressions such as "portmanteau." I suspected it had been reprinted from the 1930s. Nonetheless, it described places that sounded very appealing, most of all the Dalmatian Coast and Dubrovnik. One quote in the book cinched it. George Bernard Shaw had written, "If you want to see heaven on earth, come to Dubrovnik."

I also planned to visit Paris, and because I was going to be a psychoanalyst, I wanted to see where Sigmund Freud had lived in Vienna. Beyond that, my plans were flexible, other than the destination of Dubrovnik. Fortunately, my lowly status at the hospital made it such that when or even if I returned was of little consequence.

Although we did not realize it, by today's standards travel was difficult. Every country had its own money, border inspections, and visa requirements. Travel restrictions on cars were particularly complicated.

I had a small Hillman Husky car with an English registration. I decided to cross the channel and drive to Paris. I found a room at the City Hotel on the Île de la Cité. It is hard to believe that my room on the Quai des Orfèvres with a view of the

Rive Gauche cost less than $2.00 a night. I remember the hotel well.

My American requirement for sanitation drew me to it because it

advertised that it had a shower. Indeed, the hotel did have a shower,

but the disgruntled lady who ran the hotel could not remember

where it was located. After much searching, we discovered that it

had become a closet that stored the wet mops. For the "difficult

American," she begrudgingly cleaned it out once or twice.

After exploring Paris, I headed for Vienna. Because my

German was pretty good, I decided to travel through countries where

I knew if English failed I could rely on German. I drove through

Holland, a little of Belgium, climbed the Matterhorn in Switzerland,

and arrived in Vienna.

The Russians had only recently left Vienna and had stripped it

bare. I enthusiastically sought out Bergegasse 19, Freud's apartment

and office. I found the street and the building and asked about

Freud. Of course no one acknowledged that he lived there. I

knocked on the door of the apartment and was greeted with a surly

"Never heard of him" and a slammed door. Such was Europe in

1956.

I then drove into southern Austria having decided that I

would cross over the Karawanken Alps from Klagenfurt to Lake Bled.

Lake Bled sounded idyllic. It would be a long drive to Sarajevo, but I was fascinated to see where World War I began and had been told that I could drive south and west from Sarajevo to Dubrovnik.

Of course it was impossible to get information about road conditions. The first obstacle was finding that the pass through the Karawanken Alps had been closed by snow. At the barricade, I met a young Austrian baron looking for skiing. We talked amiably for an hour hoping the road would reopen. When he learned that I was on my way to Dubrovnik, he suggested that I drive to Villach, Austria, and down to Trieste, Italy, then an international city. He told me that from Trieste I could easily make my way to Rejika, Yugoslavia, to my confusion sometimes called by its Italian name, Fiume, leave my car, and take ferries down the Dalmatian coast. He added that his schloss was on the way to Villach and I could spend the night and leave the next morning for Trieste.

Set high on a hill, the elegant schloss had a moat, a central keep, and heavy nineteenth-century Victorian furniture. We dined on a sumptuous dinner of trout from his lake served by his elderly housekeeper. However, my leave-taking came unexpectedly early.

In the middle of the night suddenly the baron came into my bedroom ready for me to repay his kindness with my "kindness." I left hurriedly. Nonetheless, his advice was invaluable despite the price that he expected me to pay for it.

The border crossing into Yugoslavia went well, and I found myself in Rejika, a sunny, if dilapidated, Mediterranean city. There were few cars in the city, so it was not difficult to find a place to leave my car.

I found the steamer service and was told of the many islands and interesting places that dot the Dalmatian coast before reaching Dubrovnik. It was suggested that I wander at my leisure from island to island, staying as long as I wished, before catching the next ferry south.

The steamer met all my romantic notions about traveling in Europe. The sea was always still; the days were filled with bright sunshine; and the scenery was gorgeous. The boat literally wove its way through innumerable tree-covered, tiny rocky islands surrounded by deep blue waters, occasionally docking at picturesque unspoiled tiny ports. At night I slept on the moon-lit deck, often with Yugoslavian soldiers who sang the most mournful songs about lost love usually accompanied by a concertina or a harmonica. On looking back, I can hardly believe how little I carried and needed.

Everywhere, I was greeted with enthusiasm and great interest as I was the first American most had ever seen. The only other tourist was the rare unwelcome German, guiltily revisiting places where he had been during the war.

Some of the Yugoslavs spoke a little German, most having spent time as German prisoners of war. Everyone asked me about living in *Amerika* and was fascinated by my new Exakta camera. I was filled with the brazen confidence of a young American. In those days, we fancied ourselves as the liberators and the future.

I stopped several days at the ancient Roman city of Split and at several islands including Hvar and Korcula. Every exploration was rewarded a thousand fold.

After about 10 days travel on various ferries, I came into sight of Dubrovnik with its fifteenth-century opalescent white walls jutting into the turquoise sea. Much has been written about Dubrovnik in song and verse. It truly is the Pearl of the Adriatic and one of the jewels of the world.

I found a simple place to stay and quickly made friends in the numerous outdoor cafés that lined the *Stradun*--the wide promenade that bisects the completely walled city. I was an oddity but an extremely welcome oddity. Everyone wanted to talk to me.

There were few old men, and those mostly had one or two limbs missing. All the men were dressed in shabby European clothes: usually trousers, a not-very-white shirt buttoned to the neck, and the most terrible shoes I have ever seen. Women were rarely visible, but when they were, they wore black skirts, black sweaters, and a black scarf over their heads tied tightly at the chin. There were a number of young men who were boys during the war; most had escaped the war undamaged. No one seemed to have anything to do.

I met a young man about my age in a café. He told me that he had a small sailboat and asked if I would like to sail with him. With my new friend and his boat, I spent the next days exploring some of the most beautiful islands I have ever known. Largely serpentine and low-grade white marble, the islands were studded with dense pine trees growing in the crevices between marble shelves that suddenly dropped off into deep turquoise water. The swimming was marvelous.

One day, my friend asked me if I would like to go with him to the harbor to greet the first cruise ship to arrive since before the war. I found myself with a few other Yugoslavian boys diving for coins that the passengers tossed into the sea. I much enjoyed hearing some of the people on the cruise ship speaking English, calling down to us, and I pretending not to understand.

While in Dubrovnik I heard of a town called Mostar (*stari most*, old bridge), high in the hills of Herzogovina about 150 kilometers north east of Dubrovnik. I was told that it was an old Muslim community, famous for its sixteenth-century stone bridge, mill, and ancient mosques. There I might even find men still wearing *fezzes* and women in *zars* (the balloon trousers left over from the days of Turkish rule).

It was less than a 3-hour train ride, so I thought I could easily go there, see the sights, and return. For pennies I took the marvelous open air trolley from Dubrovnik over the hill to the adjacent port where I heard I could get the train.

In the station was a narrow-gauge train, easily from the late nineteenth century. I am not sure, but I think it burned wood in that the engine had a tall smoke stack. Each of the small green train cars was filled with rows of wooden benches.

On boarding, quickly I was the center of attention. I was offered all kinds of food and drink, and I was asked many questions in rudimentary German that many learned during the occupation. The questions largely concerned the way we lived in *Amerika:* what was the size of our refrigerators; was it true that we had electric stoves; are the cars as huge as they look in the movies; and the like. Repeatedly I was asked if one can see movie stars if one goes to Hollywood. I enjoyed my celebrity and spoke glowingly of our country and our desire to help the world be a better place.

The train made several stops, but my new friends made sure that I did not get off at the wrong place. The entire car was invested in my visit. When we finally arrived in Mostar, I disembarked amid many handshakes and well-wishes. As the train pulled out of the station, I took a picture of the train leaving the station as my new friends leaned out the windows waving good-bye. I was deeply touched by their desire for information and friendship.

It was a short walk from the train to the Old Bridge. I quickly became intensely involved in studying its beauty. Essentially a white stone bridge crossing an emerald river, the Neretra, the span was framed on one side by a white stone tower housing a mill that received a small side tributary and on the other by a less imposing tower. Closely aligned is a Turkish-style minaret and small mosque. I was in bliss photographing this exquisitely picturesque site, excited to think that I was perhaps the first American to visit since who knows when.

Suddenly I felt an ominous presence. To my right stood a man in rather shabby western clothes with a patch over one eye; to my left was a second man with a crutch and an empty pant leg dangling. Clearly they were *partisans,* resistance survivors of World War II who now held most of the bureaucratic positions in Yugoslavia. The man with the eye patch took my camera and camera equipment. Without a word, his head motioned that I should follow them. I knew I was in trouble.

We walked though the old section of town passing many buildings still partially rubble from the war. The streets were empty and seemed strangely quiet. We came to a nondescript cement structure, I think two stories high. Inside the two men put me into a small room with bars on the window and a wooden door with a small opening that could only be opened from the outside. In the room were a filthy cot and a bare, unlighted bulb hanging by a wire from the ceiling.

It was several hours before I heard footsteps and was taken to a larger room, equally barely furnished. In the center was a table around which sat four men--the man with the eye patch, the one-legged man, a one-armed man, and an older man. I was motioned to take a seat across from them. A very old man was brought in, whom, I thought, they treated rather roughly. He was seated next to what was obviously the head man.

The old man spoke to me in German that was barely understandable because of his thick accent. I gathered he was to be my interpreter.

They asked who I was. I explained, "I am an American studying in England." I showed them my passport and visa. That was a mistake. They immediately took it from me. I said, "I want to talk to the American Ambassador." (I later learned that we did not have an ambassador or embassy in Yugoslavia at that time.) I felt I had to be forceful but courteous. I added stiltedly, "I am a friend of Yugoslavia. I very much enjoy visiting your beautiful and wonderful land." That was also greeted with silence.

They produced my camera and my camera bag. The old man in terrible German translated the questions. "Why are you taking pictures of the railroad?" I could not believe my ears. "The railroad is a vital part of our defense force." Again I could not believe my ears. I thought "that Tooneryville Trolley is part of their military force!"

I explained again using very simple sentences, "I am enjoying your beautiful country. The people on the train were very nice to me. I took a picture of them leaning out the window and waving good-bye. I meant no harm." A long, painful silence followed.

The head man continued, "What kind of interest did the people on the train show? Tell us their questions." I replied, "Mostly questions about movie stars and cars."

I felt that things were easing. In the silence I intuited that each was afraid to take the initiative to suggest that they let me go for fear the others might report him. Finally, the head man said, "I will take the film."

Boldly and foolishly, I answered, "I won't give it to you. It has my pictures of your beautiful country on it."

Showing no knowledge of that fact that the film was an undeveloped strip of color film, the man impatiently replied, "Just give me the pictures of the train." My limitations in German made my *"Nein!"* (a word they all knew) stronger than was intended. I repeated, "It has many precious pictures on it, pictures of Split, Korcula, Hvar, Dubrovnik, the Old Bridge, and friends I have made since coming to Yugoslavia." They were taken back by my brazenness and perhaps pleased that I knew something about their country.

I moved to the offensive and said, "No one ever said that I was forbidden to take pictures of trains, and there were no signs posted." In a stroke of genius, I remembered my *A Fortnight in Yugoslavia*. I read aloud, translating into German a passage about cameras. "Do not take pictures of military installations, harbors, or radio stations." I emphasized, "You see, it says nothing about railroads."

My interrogators listened intently. There was a long silence followed by a sparse and barely audible discussion among themselves, the content of which was beyond my or my poor translator's German capabilities.

I was placed back in the cell. After what seemed an interminable period, the door opened. With a broad smile, the one-eyed man handed me my camera, intact, and my passport. He said in thickly accented English, "I hope you enjoy Yugoslavia. There is a train to Dubrovnik in about 2 hours. I will walk you to it."

I said, "You speak English. What happened?" He remained silent. My only explanation to myself was that the book, in a sense, gave the men permission to free me because no one of them had to initiate and therefore take responsibility for letting me go.

I can hardly believe it myself now, but rather than racing to freedom, I said, "I want to continue to take pictures of the Old Bridge, the mosque, and your beautiful old city. That is why I came." He nodded agreement.

I noticed that the streets were now alive with activity as I made my way with my new expert guide. Obviously when it was known that someone had been arrested, everyone hid, so great was the fear of the authorities.

We walked together, the one-eyed man and I, and he indicated that he would like me to show him my camera. He was fascinated by the lenses, the light meter, and the tripod. I opened the camera body to change the film and showed him the intricate shutter mechanism. I suggested, "Why don't you take some pictures, and I will send them to you." He shook his head, "No."

When we arrived at the train, we shook hands and I took a seat on a bench in one of the train cars. I did not take a picture of him as he waved good-bye from the platform.

On the train, I was surrounded by Yugoslavians. It was ominously quiet. One man finally said, "You are the American they arrested." I said, "How did you know that?"

"Everyone knows," he said.

He then asked, "What did they want?" I told him about the picture of the train. I said to him, "You speak English. Why didn't you come to help me?" He said, "Oh, no" and turned in silence.

I returned to Dubrovnik and my Yugoslavian friends with my story. I was something of a hero, and there was much jubilation as we drank to *A Fortnight in Yugoslavia*. The next day, as my sailing friend walked me to the ferry, he handed me an icon of St. Blaise (Sveti Vlaho), the patron saint of Dubrovnik. He said, "I don't think he would have helped much in Mostar." The icon now hangs at the foot of my analytic couch where it watches over me every day.

Embarrassed to be empty handed, I muttered, "Would you like any pictures? I will be getting them developed when I return to England." He said, "Send me one of the train and one of my boat."

I sent the pictures, but I never had a response. I do not know if he ever received them. Sometimes I have the anxious thought that maybe sending him the picture of the train was not a good idea.

1993

You cannot image the anguish I felt when on November 9, 1993, on television I saw the Old Bridge at Mostar blown up by Croatian guns.

Alone with a Psychotic

(1958)

The Department of Psychiatry at the Palo Alto Medical Clinic, Palo Alto, California, was in a small house about a block away from the clinic itself. The offices were rooms off a large living room that served as the reception and waiting area. Because I was the junior psychiatrist on the small staff, I received most of the in-take appointments and the emergency calls.

Late one afternoon I had a call from a physician who asked if I could see a man who was "acutely upset." My schedule was already full, so I told the physician to have the patient call and that I would see him that evening.

About 6:30 p.m., I received a call from a very distressed man. We spoke briefly, and I told him I could see him in my office at 8:00 p.m. It was not unusual for us to see patients in the evening, and I thought little about the fact that the building might be empty. As it turned out, I was the only one working that night.

My office was across a small hallway that led to the waiting area. At 8:00 p.m. I heard the door to the waiting area open. There in the waiting area was a little girl of about 6 years and a young man. He said, "Honey, you be good and sit here. Use your coloring book while I see the doctor." Everything seemed routine.

The young man entered my office, and we seated ourselves across from each other. He looked very frightened, but he said nothing. Quickly he was covered with sweat. I tried to make some reassuring comments when he interrupted by launching into a vitriolic tirade, "You miserable son of a bitch! I know what you are up to. You psychiatrists think everyone is crazy. You are the ones who are crazy. Don't think you deceived me. I know you gave me electric shock over the telephone. My mother had electric shock treatment. I know all about it."

I was startled and frightened. I thought, "What have I done. I am alone in this building with a crazy, wildly paranoid man--every psychiatrist's nightmare."

I tried to say quieting things, but anything I said only added to his agitation. He suddenly jumped up from his chair and began pacing around the room, pounding on the wall, shouting paranoid diatribes about psychiatrists.

At that point, the door to my office slowly opened and the little girl came in. "Daddy, Daddy, are you all right?" she cried, "Daddy, is everything all right?" She gently took his hand.

The young man picked up the little girl, returned to his chair, and placed her onto his lap. He kissed her gently and said, "Don't worry, honey. The doctor is trying to help me." He then led her back into the waiting room. He sat with her for a few minutes, helped her open her coloring book, took out some crayons, and said, "You work on this picture. We will be done soon."

He came back into the office, closed the door behind him, and again began his ranting. I was a little more composed and felt I understood better what was happening. I said, "I can tell that you are very frightened--afraid of your anger. I think you're testing me to see if your anger will frighten me off. If it did, you would have no one to help you. That terrifies you."

He put his head in his hands and began sobbing. With neither the rancor nor bluster the young man softly repeated, "You're driving me crazy." In a very controlled way, I said, "You're afraid that you are falling apart. Your feelings are tearing you to pieces. Why don't we go to the hospital? I will admit you. It will help you control yourself." He questioned quietly, "To the Looney bin?" I said, "We don't call it that, but it is the psychiatric ward. You know, it doesn't have to be like it was for your mother. Maybe we have learned more about how to help frightened people."

The young man then stood up and went back into the waiting

room. He said to the little girl, "The doctor thinks I should go to the hospital where they can help me. I'll take you to Aunt Helen's for the night."

"Will you meet me in the E.R.?" I said. He nodded agreement and picked up the little girl, kissed her, and went to his car.

After they left, I felt great relief. I was in a sweat as I realized my mistake--agreeing to meet a new patient without being sure that I was in a situation where help was available.

Slowly, I collected my belongings. As I drove to the hospital, I felt exhilaration at having skillfully handled a difficult situation. I kept thinking what one of my teachers liked to say, "No matter how crazy the behavior, it's always a communication." I thought about how relieving it was when I realized that he was testing me to see if I could tolerate his anger. It pleased me to think how much it helped him when I was able to indicate that he was fearful that his anger would drive me away and he would be alone. Clearly his rage was a defense against fear of self-fragmentation. His threatening me gave him some sense of self-cohesion. In a sense, I joined him by expressing that we are all terrified of aloneness.

The drive to the hospital was short, but I kept thinking about the strangeness of the events and the multiple riddles of schizophrenia. In my mind's eye I kept seeing him reassuring his little girl and her holding his arm. Strikingly his reassuring her and, perhaps, what I said, helped him re-compose a sense of self-cohesion.

Postscript

The young man was admitted to the hospital. In those days, we did not have much in the way of medication. The only tools we had for dealing with terrifying ideas and feelings were being available and providing understanding--powerful tools not to be underestimated.

My intuitions about this man were confirmed. His greatest fear was that it was inevitable that he would be like his deeply depressed, episodically and frequently psychotic mother. Even more he feared his continuing rage at her for being left by her during her frequent hospitalizations when he was a child. The rage at her could not be expressed for fear of driving her further into insanity and an even more terrifying aloneness--the aloneness of his being with her but her not being psychologically there.

Lost in the Desert

(1966)

It does not seem that 1966 should be a long time ago, but it is. The world was much larger then, and trip planning to anywhere other than the most-visited places was difficult at best. Letters took 2 weeks to be delivered (if they were at all), and 2 weeks to be answered, overseas telephone calls were expensive and hard to arrange, fax machines had yet to be invented, and of course there was nothing as easily available and instant as e-mail.

It was in Spring 1966 that Evie and I embarked on an extensive trip to the Middle East to visit in Iran my old college roommate and closest friend. The fact that he was a prince of the Qajar dynasty and that we had spent many hours talking about his extraordinary family, many of whom I now knew, made the visit more compelling. The plan was to visit Egypt, Israel, Iran, and Turkey. I also much wanted to add a stop in Jordan to see the "rose-red city" of Petra.

Dwarfing any difficulties in communications was the fact that the world was, as now, in much turmoil. The situation in the Middle

East was, as now, even worse. Most of Jerusalem was in Jordan, and Israel and Jordan were technically at war. We could not fly directly from Egypt to Israel. Concern was also great about the contents of one's passport and which visas and stamps it contained.

Our plan was to start from Italy, where we could take a short flight to Egypt for 2 weeks. We could then easily fly from Egypt to Jordan, which would allow a much desired visit to the old city of Jerusalem, other places in the Holy Land under Jordanian control, a visit to Petra, and the adventure of walking though the Mandelbaum Gate into Israel. Because Iran was not at war with Israel, we could fly from Tel Aviv, Israel, to Teheran, Iran, and then from Teheran to Ankara, Turkey. From Ankara we planned to take the famed Orient Express to Istanbul, and from there return to San Francisco. The trip was daring, exciting, and risky, but doable.

Because of the discord among and in these countries, Evie had more trepidation than I. At least she expressed it more. Reluctantly she agreed to the plan even though everyone discouraged us from the endeavor. I was determined. Visiting my old college friend in Iran was worth any discomfort and risk.

The trip began badly. The layover in Italy was a good idea; however, we missed our flight to Cairo and were booked on a Middle East Airlines flight. To my horror, it turned out to be a Comet, the first passenger jet airplane, long since abandoned because of mid-air explosions. We were not reassured when we were told that it would be flown at a low altitude and at a reduced speed.

Arriving in Egypt, with her beautiful olive complexion, dark eyes, tiny figure, and dark hair, Evie was an instant success. In fact she was an instant success in each of the countries we visited: Italy, Egypt, Jordan, Israel, Iran, and Turkey. In each country people attempted to talk to her in their native language and welcomed her back as if she were coming home. In each country I stuck out like a sore thumb with my graying blond hair, blue eyes, and under the Middle Eastern sun ever-pinkening skin. Although I was filled with excitement in seeing the great monuments of Egypt, I found myself fascinated by the arid vastness of the desert. In a curious way, in Egypt I felt that I had returned.

The Arab men were especially excited by my beautiful wife. Everywhere we went we were treated with extraordinary courtesy and privilege. This was an advantage because travel in Egypt was nearly impossible. Although our visit to the Upper Nile and Cairo was a grand adventure, everywhere confusion reined supreme, nowhere more than at the Cairo Airport. The fact that we actually got onto a United Arab Air flight from Cairo to Amman, Jordan, was nothing short of a miracle.

This miracle took the form of the United Arab Air pilot who spotted us and remembered that he had piloted us from Cairo to Luxor, Egypt, a flight on the most decrepit DC-3 I had ever seen. On that trip, the pilot attempted to reassure us by saying that he used to fly for Pan American. It was only during the flight that Evie got up the courage to ask me, "I wonder why he isn't still flying for Pan Am?"

Fortunately, our new friend, the pilot, saw us struggling in the Cairo airport and proudly announced that he was piloting us to Amman. With great aplomb and dispatch he ushered us through the morass that was supposed to be lines and escorted us onto an even-more-decrepit DC-6 than the earlier DC-3. Traveling in the Arab countries in those days was a lesson in aviation history.

Our friend escorted us to our seats. Evie attempting to make causal conversation asked, "Will we see Mt. Sinai on the flight?" "I will make sure you do," he answered. We did not know that that meant he would fly off course to circle the mountain nor that he would invite us into the cockpit and insist that Evie take his place at the controls of the plane as we swept low "for the perfect view." Serendipity has its disadvantages.

Amman proved to be a dingy, crowded desert town with but one international hotel, the Philadelphia, from which we could make arrangements for the long-dreamed-of visit to Petra. Amman itself had little else to offer.

The best way to visit Petra was to hire a taxicab from Amman to Wadi Musa, an oasis in the valley associated with the Exodus tale of Moses's striking a rock and miraculously bringing forth water. The idea of walking where Moses walked added greatly to our excitement. Throughout the trip we were in agreement that we would not be skeptics. We were determined, at least temporarily, to regard as history the traditional sites attributed to the Old and New Testament events that were everywhere in Jordan and Israel.

Shortly after midnight, in a battered old taxi, we headed southwest over desert terrain far more barren than that of southwestern Wyoming and Nevada. The only signs of humanity were several abandoned remnants of the Haj railroad, conjuring memories of T.E. Lawrence of Arabia and the occasional Bedouin with a make-shift tent tending a flock of sheep or goats. Both reminded us of the mythical romance that surrounds the desert.

After driving over 3 hours on a narrow asphalt road, we reached Wadi Musa deep in the Wadi Arba, the great valley that runs from the Dead Sea to the Gulf of Aqaba. The oasis turned out to be nothing more than a small wooden hut covered by a metal roof and a few tools to repair cars next to a large rock from which trickled a small spring that fed a few scrubby trees. In this vast moonscape, the spring and the trees indeed were a miracle.

At the oasis, we were met by two Bedouins wearing caftans and the typical red-checked *kuffiyeh* held by the double-corded black *igal* that Jordanian men wrap around their heads and dramatically drape over their shoulders. With them were two small horses. The men spoke no English, but they greeted us with broad smiles accented by several gold among many missing teeth. It was hard to tell their age. Their bodies were thin like teenagers, but their faces were deeply lined by the desert wind and sun.

They held the horses while we mounted, and through motions they indicated that at times we would have to bring our legs up over the top of the saddle when the path was excessively narrow. The cab driver, attempting to reassure his anxious fares, told us that we need not worry about the flash floods that sometimes rush through the canyon because they were rare at this time of year. "Flash floods!" I thought. "What flash floods?"

Our Bedouin guides led the horses by their bridles, walking quickly, sometimes trotting, beside us. Soon we came to a narrow opening in the side of a cliff, the entrance to this magical place. It was then that we entered the *syk* (Arabic for shaft), an unbelievably narrow gorge that runs between the sandstone cliffs and connects the main desert to the Petra Valley. Two miles long, with sides looming nearly 350 feet into the sky and a path that is often less than 8 feet wide, the syk was eerily dark, cold, and arid. Brush growing out of the walls further narrowed the path, and our guides frequently tapped our legs to remind us to hoist them over the neck of the horse to allow passage.

Swipes and swirls of sandstone marked the walls and rocks in vivid demonstration of the power of past rushes of water down this narrow passage. At times, claustrophobic panic accompanied our remembering the cab driver's "reassurance" that flash floods *only rarely* occurred during this time of year.

As dawn burst, we came upon a brightly lighted opening. Before us, carved from brilliant red and delicate yellow sandstone, was the facade of a three-story classical Roman building. As we moved into the opening, we found ourselves standing before the 2,000-year-old Al Kazneh, the Treasury. The drabness of the desert at Wadi Musa and the darkness of the syk dramatically enhanced the unreal quality of the vision.

Although much historical documentation, speculation, and mythology exists about the origins of this ancient site, we chose for ourselves a romantic version, greatly influenced by John William Burgon's 1845 poem *Petra,* a poem chiefly known for its couplet

Match me such marvel save in Eastern clime

A rose-red city half as old as time!

Ignoring the vast complexity of the history and architecture of Petra, we chose the version that ties Petra to the love affair between Caesar and Cleopatra. That story begins with the valley as an ancient stronghold of the Nabataeans from which they raided the vital trade routes between the Orient and Europe. Rooted out by Caesar, the valley was taken over by his legions to protect this vital trade passageway. Legend has it that the soldiers, during their idle time, carved the magnificent Roman-style facades on the existing Nabataean caves.

The daunting syk provided clear evidence as to how successfully hidden was this curiosity of the world, a treasure known in the Middle Ages but essentially rediscovered by Western eyes only early in the nineteenth century. The jewel-like quality of this small valley with its central oasis and soaring cliffs of red and yellow sandstone carved into magical Roman facades gave credence to the myth that Caesar gave Petra to Cleopatra as a wedding gift.

In the center of this incredible setting was an ugly, two-story square cement building euphemistically called "The Hotel." On entering it, we found a shabbily dressed clerk sitting at a make-shift desk. Without a smile, he asked, "Do you want a room or a cave?"

Timidly we admitted that we preferred a room and were taken to a barrack-style bare room with two cot-like beds that was illuminated by a single exposed light bulb hanging from the ceiling. However, through the small window we could see an entire wall of carved facades.

We immediately set out to explore the valley, climbing around the facades that are elaborate "doorways" leading to small, bare interior caves. These caves housed the Nabataeans and later the Roman legionnaires. A few of the caves were outfitted with cots, the other rooming choice offered by our "hotel." They housed backpacking youngsters from a variety of European nations who were our only other fellow travelers.

Darkness came early and completely to the valley when the generators were turned off at 9:00 p.m. We stared spellbound into the night sky at the blaze of stars and the darting comets. Brightly lit and seemingly close to the Earth, it were as though we could scoop them up into a bucket. No wonder that nomadic people of the desert in lore and myth were always close to the stars.

Sleep came quickly, and we were up before dawn eager to explore the valley before the hot noon sun would be upon us. The sunrise was magnificent, and Burgon's "rose-red city" at dawn was indeed that.

We had heard that there was a magnificent building, El Dier, The Monastery, about 4 miles up a steep mountain trail. The hotel clerk told us that from El Dier we could see Jabal Haroun (Mt. Hor) topped by the tomb of Aaron, Moses's brother.

The hotel clerk assured us that no guide was necessary because the trail was easy to follow. Needless to say, we greeted the adventure with eager anticipation.

So, up we climbed. Once off the valley floor, the landscape was dry desert with scrub brush. The path narrowed, and before long we lost sight of the valley below. We also lost the path and found ourselves amid a maze of goat trails. We forged ahead, thinking it best to go up, but with complete disorientation. Unspoken was the fear that we were lost in the desert.

We knew that the belligerence between Jordan and Israel continued, and we had heard stories of brave Israeli youths who boasted of having crossed the border to see Petra. We also had heard of those who had been shot on sight.

We walked for about an hour when suddenly a Bedouin sporting criss-crossed bandoleers with cartridges and a rifle jumped down from a rock in front of our path. We were terrified as he motioned with his head that we should follow him. There was no question about what we should do. I feared he was a Jordanian border guard taking us captive.

We followed him in silence. Suddenly he stopped short, took bullets from his bandoleers, and loaded his gun. I was sure that he was going to shoot us on the spot.

To our astonishment, he took careful aim down a ravine and shot a bird. With a smile he handed his rifle to Evie to hold while he climbed down the ravine to retrieve his dinner. I think Evie was more frightened holding the loaded gun than she was when we were sure that we were to be executed.

We continued our silent march up and up until we came to a large clearing, and there we beheld the magnificent red stone carved facade of El Dier. Our would-be assassin was the monument's guard. Evidently he had spotted us on his way to work. Accurately sensing that we were lost, he came to our rescue. Unbelievably, that was to be only the *first* time that he rescued me that day.

A 150-foot Roman temple facade in deep red and orange hues, El Dier is somewhat box-like. Its two tiers are divided by a deep cornice. The lower tier is a series of Ionic columns holding triangular porticoes; the upper tier, three rectangular structures with columns and porticos. Topping the structure is a large dome and finial. Emboldened by having found this sacred place and having it all to ourselves, I decided that I would climb to the top of the finial of the central dome.

With camera around my neck and without difficulty, I made my way up the carved surface to the central dome. Climbing on the curved surface of the dome posed difficulty until I was able to stand holding onto the finial. Once on the top, I had a magnificent view. In the distance I saw the mosque marking Aaron's tomb. What a glorious feeling--until I decided that it was time to descend.

Because of the curvature of the dome, I could not see a way down. I was panic stricken. I feared leaning out, but clutching the finial made it impossible to see how to proceed.

I yelled to Evie far below. The panic in my tone spoke more than what I said. Within seconds, our once-thought-of executioner, the Bedouin, was at my side. He motioned for me to get on my hands and knees. Like the good mother leading a baby, he guided me down the side of the dome.

My gratitude was boundless, and yet I had no words to express what I felt. I reached into my wallet and brought out some $20.00 bills. He turned his back on me and disappeared. In moments, he reappeared and indicated that I should hold out my hand. In it he placed a small ancient Roman oil lamp and walked away.

I was dumbstruck. I knew that something important had

transpired. By this time a lone backpacker appeared. He said that he knew the way back, and when he was ready the three of us descended in silence.

Back at the hotel, I talked to the manager and explained what had happened. I told him that I wanted to leave some money for my savior. Rather abruptly he said, "Impossible!" In the overly formal way that Arabs often speak English, he said, "In our way, when you save the life of a man, you are indebted to him for life for you have deprived him of the blessing of going to Heaven. The only way to break the indebtedness is to give the man a present. That is why he gave you the oil lamp--so he will not be indebted to you."

It was at a certain level and only partially that my Western mind could understand that reasoning. That oil lamp remains one of my most cherished possessions. To think I will never even know the young man's name.

The Afternoon I Died in Vienna

(1975)

Following World War II it took many years for Vienna to recover from the physical and intellectual loss it suffered under the Nazis. Psychoanalysis was among the last lost treasures to be re-discovered.

Psychoanalysis in Vienna began its rebirth when a few older Viennese psychoanalysts, who had been forced to leave, slowly returned. By the early 1950s, a small new generation of Viennese joined the returning group and psychoanalysis in Vienna began its second infancy. It is hard for me to believe that 36 years after the death of Sigmund Freud, I helped reintroduce psychoanalysis to Vienna.

Like so many events in one's life, my connection with Vienna came about as the result of a curious circumstance. In the 1960s, Arnold Schmidt, a distinguished Viennese physicist, was awarded a 1-year visiting professorship at the University of California, Berkeley. His wife, Catherine, a physician and neurophysiologist, accompanied him. A woman of unusual beauty, charm, and intellect, Kitty, as we called her, immediately began looking for places to study in the San Francisco Bay Area during their stay. She happened upon the Mt. Zion Hospital Psychiatric Clinic in San Francisco where I conducted a case conference on psychoanalytically oriented psychotherapy that, over the years, had achieved some renown. She became an eager and excellent participant in that seminar, immersing herself in the psychoanalytic perspective. She also began attending my dream seminar at the San Francisco Psychoanalytic Institute. Because we in the United States had essentially grown up with the psychoanalytic perceptive, it was hard to realize how new and wondrous the ideas seemed to her.

On the Schmidts' return to Vienna, we, now good friends, parted with hopes that our friendship would continue. Nonetheless, I was surprised a year or two later to receive a telephone call from Kitty. She asked if I would come to Vienna to give a lecture on psychoanalysis.

Pleased and honored, I asked, "Kitty, what should I talk about?" Without a moment's thought, she exclaimed, "Dreams!" I was dumbfounded. How could it be that a boy from the western plains of Wyoming would be asked to lecture on dreams in Vienna?

When Evie and I arrived in Vienna, we were astonished at the interest in the work and the cordiality offered by Kitty, Arnold, and

their colleagues and friends. I soon learned that the lecture was to
be a public lecture at the University of Vienna and that it had been
advertised that it would be in English. I was sure that no one would
come. To my surprise, the auditorium was full with a standing-room-
only crowd. It was a great success. After the lecture, it was arranged
that I would begin regular visits at the university and teach in their
developing psychoanalytic institute.

I asked my new colleagues, "Why are you inviting someone
who is limited in German? There are many American psychoanalysts
whose mother tongue is German." I was told, "We want to learn
about these things in English. The German language has changed,
and psychoanalytic theory has changed. The most important
influence is American. When the older psychoanalysts come, they
speak an older German and use older concepts. We want to learn in
English so we can master the new literature."

What seemed a straightforward reason turned out to be
far more complex. Being naïve and full of enthusiasm, my visits
to Vienna were always stimulating and enjoyable. I was to go to
Vienna many times before I fully sensed the factions and conflicts
in that fledging psychoanalytic community between the young and
the old, between the newly returned and those who had never left.
Unbeknownst to me, to a certain degree I became the center of some

of these conflicts. To my astonishment I realized that I was being identified with the new psychoanalysis.

Always my colleagues were eager to learn about the theory and the techniques of psychoanalytically oriented psychotherapy and how psychoanalytic theory had developed in the years since Freud left Vienna in 1938. Always the participants were courteous and somewhat diffident. I was *Herr Docktor Professor.* Yet any attempt on my part to dodge a question or get by with an ambiguity was directly, though courteously, challenged. Deep and lasting friendships rapidly formed.

Working between languages, in a different culture, and with "students" who were eager learners sharpened my thoughts and my psychoanalytic lexicon. Often they apologized for their accent as they struggled for an English word or phrase. I found this amusing. One time I commented, "In the United States, everyone has an accent. If we don't, most likely our parents do. If our parents don't, certainly our grandparents did." I reminded them that most of my teachers in psychoanalysis sounded just like they did.

At first, the cases sounded unfamiliar. The patients typically began with "My father was killed on the Western Front." I noted with my new colleagues that in the United States the cases usually began, "My parents divorced when I was 3." With time, the feeling of cultural difference lessened, and the universality of core conflicts supervened. Clearly only the language and specifics were different.

We often met all day long with wonderful coffees, long lunches, and beautiful dinners. Evening meetings began at 10:00 p.m. and continued to midnight. Although Americans are used to working hard and rigorous schedules, I must confess that the Viennese frequently wore me out.

Evie and I liked staying at the beautiful Hotel im Schwarzenberg Palais, an eighteenth-century palace that was the summer residence of the Schwarzenberg family and continued as the Vienna residence of Prince Schwarzenberg. The Schwarzenberg occupied 18 acres of garden and is adjacent to the baroque Schlöss Belvedere and the Belvedere gardens. Although at some distance from Vienna's center and the university, we enjoyed the quiet beauty of the area and the Old World charm that the hotel maintained.

The rooms were huge and overly Victorian with heavy red velvet draperies, marble-topped commodes, and chaise lounges. The room I particularly liked had a magnificent view of the vast gardens of the Schwarzenberg and the Belvedere.

On one of our visits, Evie had to return early, and I remained on alone. One particularly grueling day was followed by a late evening seminar. The next day there was a morning seminar, a long lunch, and an early afternoon seminar. At a point, I had to explain to my gracious hosts that I just had to have a nap. With much apologizing, they returned me to the hotel, and I collapsed into the magnificent, oversized bed.

Instantly I fell into a deep, dreamless sleep. I have no idea how long I had been asleep when I was awakened by celestial music. Half awake and half asleep, I felt engulfed by the deep red velvet draperies surrounding the bed, the lace-trimmed pillows, and the white padded silk comforter.

Lying very still, I heard voices singing. I had a startling thought. I had died and was lying in a deeply cushioned, red velvet casket listening to angels. I thought, "If this is death, it isn't that bad. In fact it's like it is in the movies." I awakened a little more, and the angelic voices were even more distinct.

I bolted upright. Unsure of where I was, I staggered over to the window. It was a gloriously sunny day. In the garden were the angels--over 50 of them in dark blue Edwardian sailor suits. The Vienna Boys Choir was serenading the hotel.

A Western Psychoanalyst Visits an Ancient Hindu Temple[1]

(1979)

During several visits to India, I noted how difficult it was to convey my impressions of a Hindu temple to my Indian colleagues, Muslim and Hindu alike. I believed this was due to the fact that for an Indian a Hindu temple is a fact of life--something taken for granted. On returning home, I found it even more difficult, if not impossible, to describe the experience to my Western colleagues. The multitude of complex sights and activities, seen, heard, and smelled, that comprise the Hindu temple are so alien to Western concepts and experience that it is impossible to convey through ordinary words.

After innumerable futile attempts, impeded by innumerable color slides, I discovered the right word to connote the experience. With colleagues, Western and Eastern alike, I finally could make contact when I said simply, "It is like a dream."

The Great Temple of Meenakshi-Sudareswarar

After several visits in Northern India, in 1979 Evie and I decided to make a long and difficult excursion by car deeply into

---

1   The original version of this essay was printed in *SAMIKSA*, the Journal of the Indian Psychoanalytical Society, 1980, Vol. 34, No. 2.

southern India to the Tamil Nadu to visit Hindu temples. The climax of the trip was the great temple of Meenakshi-Sundareswarar at Madurai, a temple complex near the very southern apex of that fantastic subcontinent.

In India, there are literally tens of thousands of Hindu temples of varying size, significance, age, and devotional practices. In my mind, I keep a composite of the score that we visited; however, the experience was epitomized in the extraordinary Meenakshi-Sudareswarar.

The Meenakshi is of great size and renown. Its origins are ancient. Though not particularly distinctive for artistic treasures, it is a "living" Hindu temple in the fullest sense of that word.

The temple commemorates the transformation and marriage of two deities. This marriage is spoken of in the most literal way by the guides in the temple and by the Indian friends whom we met during our visit. It was only after some time that I realized that "marriage" to the Indian mind denotes the co-union of two highly anthropomorphized theological abstractions symbolizing the end of a great ideological and, I assumed, political difference.

I don't know enough about the history of the temple to detail the strife that was ended by this ecumenical gesture. What I do know is how vividly the end of a great political-theological struggle becomes when conceptualized as a marriage; and how meaningful a temple becomes when seen as the commemoration of such an event. Clearly the temple's very name, like every aspect of the temple, like all Hindu temples, is an extraordinary metaphorical composite made visual. It is like a dream.

A Passage into a Dream-Like Space

Western religious structures instill a concept of outside versus inside. Typically our great sacred edifices are approached by mounting flights of stairs to enormous portals that penetrate soaring walls. No matter how vaulting the ceiling, entering is entering into an enclosed space.

By contrast, the typical Hindu temple is on the same level as the outside. Entry is through mammoth and elaborate *gopurams* (portals). However, the gopurams are not entrances through walls but rather gigantic symbols of passing through. The temple is a series of portals, courtyards, and pavilions of various heights, united under the open sky. The act of entering becomes a sequential movement into a different space and a different realm defying the dichotomy of outside and inside. It is places within a place and worlds within the world. Like a dream, the Hindu temple condenses the familiar, the arcane, and the esoteric.

My Visit

There is indeed a Western reluctance to removing one's shoes and stockings on entering a common area. Western aesthetics are quite co-mingled with sanitation. Yet we easily shake hands with strangers, something a Hindu would never do, even with a friend.

Boldly, I placed my bare feet against the stone temple floor. I felt at once apart from (perhaps that Western sanitary wish to be apart from?) and united with humanity. At first, I futilely tried to avoid the varieties of dung and other things as I walked. But before long my aversions gave way, and I could feel primal desires mixed with fleeting memories of the delights of being a barefoot child. What before resulted in being scolded now at last not only was condoned, but required. The experience was made all the more profound because a recent rain left its mark, and I happily went barefoot through the puddles.

For the Westerner, the permanent living inhabitants of the Hindu temple are from the land of dreams: monkeys flying overhead; screeching, vividly colored birds; wandering cows; the occasional camel; and most of all the sacred elephant, ornately painted, blessing those who gave him the proper coin with a not-so-gentle thump on the head with his trunk.

Even more fascinating are the temple's symbolic inhabitants--

the flagrant display of innumerable, massed polychromatic statues. Everywhere, representations of human beings, fully expressing visually an incalculable array of every conceivable antic, inhabit a world of phantasmagorical creatures and anthropomorphic animals. As I perused the array, I realized how restricted visual representation has become for the Western mind reflecting our 6,000-year reluctance toward the graven image.

At first, I was to be taken aback by the panoply of representations. I tried to regain a modicum of control by depreciating what I saw, labeling it gaudy, grotesque, and Disneyland-like. Gradually, I became fascinated by the multiheaded demons, females with necklaces of skulls, celestial lovers riding on birds of paradise, floating dancers, musicians, decapitating creatures, hags, ethereal beauties, suckling babies, and hermaphroditic forms. Overcoming a tendency to repress visual sexual forms, I began to appreciate the visual representation of the full sexual pleasure of exploring the complementarity of the male and female body. As I more fully integrated what I saw, I began to realize that I was experiencing a commemorative celebration of the totality of being human, a visual, metaphorical portrayal of every aspect of the vagrancy and the nobility of humankind.

The vast array of allegorical forms was complemented by the

transient visitors to the temple. The thousands of devotees who visit the Meenakshi each day would be an oppressive sight if it were not that as a people they are small, compact, dark, fine featured, with flashing eyes and bright white teeth, colorfully attired, and have a natural grace. Counterbalancing the health and vitality of the visitors was the cadre of beggars--maimed lepers, sufferers of elephantiasis, and blinded starving deformed creatures of every conceivable description, practicing their ancient art as they played on the guilt and fear of the well. Somewhere between were the *sadhus,* the naked holy men dressed only in ashes, directed by an inner quest. The aura was made all the more surreal by the fleeting glimpses of monks and priests who quietly moved in and out of sanctuaries, their faces vividly painted to denote their sect, and their small, lithe, dark bodies accentuated by fuchsia or saffron robes, or a simple white loin cloth.

Striking was the lack of corporate ritual. I was reminded that there is no aloneness so complete as spiritual aloneness as one watches within a seething multitude, a worshipper, ritualistically bobbing, barely audibly chanting, or serenely mediating in silent prayer.

The great spiritual intensity in the temple in the midst of a vernacular ambiance of laughing, talking, meandering, buying, haggling, and gossiping, coupled with the ringing, clanging, and whine of the temple musicians with an occasional colorful, awesome, arcane procession of worshippers and idols made it clear that I was in the middle of a people spiritually and temporally experiencing dimensions that Westerners have compartmentalized into art, religion, and dreaming. As Eric Erikson wrote in *Gandhi's Truth* (1969) "Indians, I believe, live in more centuries at the same time than most other peoples." I would add it seemed to me that the Hindu temples, like India itself, represented a microcosmic composite condensation of all that is eternally human of every epoch and era. I felt like I was watching humanity in unaging action.

An Epiphany--the Lingam *and the* Yoni

The Siva temple, of which the Meenakshi is one, had a special significance in store for the Western psychoanalyst. I felt a heightened curiosity with intensifying excitement as I moved toward the *sanctum sanctorium* (the holy of the holies). As I watched the worship of the *lingam* (the abstract representation of Siva's phallus), like in the dream, the symbol became simultaneously abstract and strikingly concrete. I realized that I was witnessing a pure appreciation of the power of the phallus with its most atavistic magical connotations. I was astonished to see it decorated with garlands of flowers and bathed with holy ointment by men and women alike, ritualistically genuflecting before the awesome stone symbol. I realized that the representation was even more complex as I fully acknowledged the circle of flowers at the base of the *lingam* outlining the *yoni* (the circular base on which the lingam stands), the "female principle."

I gazed at the constellation of the lingam on the yoni innumerable times trying to make psychoanalytic sense out of the curious juxtaposition of the phallus centrally placed on the yoni platform. I knew that in ritualistic matters, like in the dream, no element is incomplete, redundant, a matter of chance, or ambiguous. At first I was convinced that the complex represented the ancient protection against castration, the phallication of the female genitalia. Somehow I knew that my interpretation more reflected familiar theory than what was represented, for I had already been struck by the Indian full acknowledgement, acceptance, and portrayal of the essential bisexuality of the human being.

Reflecting on the form as a condensation of images like in a dream, I had an epiphany. Suddenly I understood the peculiar placement of the lingam centrally on the yoni. It seemed clear that in the spiritual center of the temple, the Holy of the Holies, I was looking down upon the phallus in the vagina. It was as though I were in the womb looking on the erect phallus ringed at its base by the introitus. It suddenly occurred to me that the center of Siva worship was not of the phallus, as is widely held, but rather in a way at once abstract and concrete, the center of worship was the moment of creation itself.

I came to realize that being in a Hindu temple was experiencing as a composite totality all aspects and attributes of the agony and ecstasy of being human--from birth to death and before birth and after death--depicted in exquisite visual allegory. If my experience and understanding can be generalized, I suggest that the Hindu temple is a celebration of life itself. The Sivite has chosen to intensify in this celebration the mystical moment of conception. Like the conception of the child, the lingam in the yoni celebrates the moment that all that has been is transformed into all that will be.

The Mexican Weaver and Miró

(1984)

It was to be a family vacation. Evie and I decided that it was time to show the children the wonders of Mexico. I have always felt that one can travel a lot further than Mexico and see a lot less.

It was Christmas time, and our older daughter, Cici, was able to take time from her job as an editor. Noah, a senior at Stanford University, was on holiday and eager for an adventure, and our younger daughter, Annalisa, a junior at Tufts University was ready to leave behind the snows of Boston for some sunshine and would meet us in Mexico City.

Mexico offered the right mixture of history, culture, and pleasure for our family. The plan was to see Mexico City and its National Museum of Anthropology, travel to the beautiful colonial city of Oaxaca and explore nearby Monte Alban, and end our travels at the beach in Puerto Vallarta, then a sleepy fishing village on the Pacific Ocean. The trip held the promise of a perfect mixture. The children would learn about Mexican culture and history, experience its fascinating history, try to use a foreign language, study native arts and crafts, and enjoy a beautiful beach.

In Oaxaca, we were lucky enough to enjoy the Camino Real Hotel, a former convent, close to the *zócalo* (town square). The visits to Monte Alban proved an excellent addition to what we had learned in the National Museum of Anthropology. The children quickly became interested in the crafts that are everywhere in Mexico and enthusiastically joined us as we prowled the markets looking at weavings, carvings, and pottery. We were particularly impressed with the quality and variety of the weaving, especially in Oaxaca, which was a center for that craft.

Inquiry revealed that in the hills surrounding Oaxaca lived many weavers who would bring their wares to town on market days. We were told that we could visit some of these remote weavers in their villages and watch the processing of the wool, the dying, and the weaving. After some investigation, we learned of an outstanding weaver living high in the mountains. We were warned that travel to his village was difficult and required a four-wheel drive vehicle.

We eagerly set out to find this man and his village. We passed through several tiny villages that were little more than clusters of hovels and huts with a few mangy goats and the occasional cow. In these villages, our arrival was an event, and children came out running to smile and wave as we passed.

After several hours of travel over dusty, rutted roads, much enjoying the wild rugged splendor, we arrived at our destination. We had little difficulty finding our weaver as his village was also but a few huts. He spoke no English and only rudimentary Spanish. We recognized the harsh sounds of one of Mexico's many indigenous dialects as he called his wife and children. Using motions, he invited us into his hut. I spotted an unusual rug hanging from a rafter. I could not believe my eyes. On its white background, in a checkerboard array of colors, was a strong anthropomorphic form. Below the form was a large red circle with a half-formed, curious, tilted face-like image jutting to one side. In the margins were black tendril-like flares, often ending in star bursts. For all the world, it looked like a painting by Joan Miró.

I could hardly contain myself. Here in the remote mountains of the Sierra Madre del Sur, I had found evidence that might solve a riddle that early on galvanized psychoanalysis.

Carl Jung strongly held that the similarities in primitive artistic representations transcending culture evidence a common atavistic ancestry, a racial unconscious and a racial memory. Sigmund Freud, less inclined toward such sweeping and untestable ideas, was dubious.

Although I inclined toward the Freudian, I had to admit

that finding a weaver, living and working in such desolate isolation, searching for inspiration only within himself, who was manifesting forms identical to Miró's whimsical, yet suggestively archaic ones, strongly favored Jung's position. Excitedly I thought, "I have found strong evidence for a common, inherited memory."

I could hardly contain myself as I pointed to the hanging rug. The weaver inquiringly responded, "The Miró?"

Michelangelo's God and I

(1988)

It was in St. Peter's Basilica, Rome, in 1977 that I was first struck with how a psychoanalytic way of looking at things, to use Erik Erickson's perceptive phrase, can change one's appreciation of art. It had been a long time since I had been in Rome, and it was Evie's first visit. Being new in psychoanalysis, I wanted to see Michelangelo's *Moses* statue because I had studied and taught Sigmund Freud's essay on the colossus. I was struck by how much Freud saw in the statue. I sensed early that psychoanalysis could teach much about the art piece as well as about the artist, an idea that underlies much of my writing about psychoanalysis as an important complement to art history.

In the Vatican, we rushed to see the Sistine Chapel. I remember being awestruck by the distant, Byzantine murkiness of the ceiling panels, and I confess to having scarcely noticed the great fifteenth-century murals below. Moving quickly on to St. Peter's, we found Michelangelo's *Pietà*. In those days of innocence, the *Pietà* was on a pedestal just above eye level in the center of the small Villiers Chapel. One could leisurely walk around it.

The guidebook mentioned the inordinate youthfulness of Mary, noting that she was younger than the dead Christ. I remembered the explanation. Using a quote from Michelangelo's response to contemporary criticism, the guidebook explained that in Michelangelo's depiction of Mary as child-like he was depicting her as "unsullied" by life's travail. The book went on to describe related theological explanations regarding her purity.

I knew fairly little about Michelangelo at the time, but such explanations seemed only partial. I did know that Michelangelo was separated at birth from his mother because of her illness and was reared by a wet-nurse in Settignano, a village near Florence, Italy, until he was about 3 years old. (Both art historians and psychoanalysts make much of the fact that his wet-nurse was the wife and daughter of stone cutters.) I also knew that Michelangelo's mother died when he was about 6 years old and that his father was not to remarry until Michelangelo was in his early teens. As an epiphany, it seemed to me that in the *Pietà* Michelangelo depicted a mother who never aged. In that sense the statue was autobiographical.

I began exploring at length the *pietà* theme, the dead Christ being returned to the body of His mother, and the youthfulness of the mother. More specifically it seemed to me that at a deeper level, the *pietà* theme evokes, enhanced by Michelangelo in his statue, the archetypical wish to be returned to the mother of our infancy.

With the help of a fortuitous photograph of the sculpture from an aerial perspective, I could see that the statue was essentially a circle, with the young Mary occupying half of the circle and the dead Jesus forming an overlapping but not bisecting whole. When viewed from above, the two figures essentially become the archetypical Yin-Yang symbol. Using the mystery of the circle, the end that is a beginning, Michelangelo's St. Peter's *Pietà* depicts the eternal cycle of death and rebirth, resurrection in its most abstract form.

This revelation led me to countless hours of pleasure as I studied Michelangelo's other *pietàs* in Rome, Florence, and Milan. Over the years the work led me to write several psychoanalytic papers on the *pietàs* providing some prestige in the developing world of the psychoanalytic appreciation of art and artists. The work gave me access to fascinating people studying fascinating ideas.

By 1979, I felt my work on Michelangelo to be complete until I made another visit to the Vatican. I was dumbfounded when I viewed the Sistine Chapel through more knowledgeable eyes.

I was aware of the frequently presented idea that there is a marked difference in scale between the three panels of *The Histories* closer to the entrance than the panels closer to the altar. In studying art psychoanalytically, I had long learned to mistrust explanations about "errors" by great masters. Who of instance can accept that Michelangelo's giant *David* in Florence has disproportionately large hands and feet when everyone knows that the hands and feet of male adolescents grow first and though seeming disproportionate in fact portend their strength and power? Michelangelo's *David* shows us like a composite the David who is *and* the David who will be.

Guided by the great interpreter of Michelangelo, Charles de Tolnay, I became interested in a palinodal interpretation that the Sistine Ceiling's *Histories* suggested. Viewed entrance to altar, I felt that because of their larger size, the early events from the myth of *Creation* (the panels nearer the altar) became integral to the later events (the panels over the entrances) of humankind. Considered psychoanalytically, in the panels, as in a dream, the past becomes visibly condensed into the present with earlier events looming larger and ever effecting later events. The sequence in the panels entrance to altar becomes a visualization of the ontological recapitulation of the development of the individual with the past residing within the present. Entering into the chapel and looking back from the altar, the vision, told through the metaphor of the biblical texts, is of the lengthy linear road necessary for the human animal to become a human being.

This weighty idea took many years to reach verification through study of the history of the Sistine Chapel, the interacting themes and figures in the Sistine Ceiling, and the interaction among and with the narratives of the fifteenth-century murals that line the walls. The verification was largely guided by the psychoanalytic understanding of the structure of the dream and personality development.

The laborious study, published as *Michelangelo's Sistine Ceiling, A Psychoanalytic Study of Creativity* (1989), took more years to complete than the 4 years it took Michelangelo to paint the Sistine Ceiling. Those years were filled with exciting discoveries and rewarding contacts with experts working in many different fields. The work gave me fascinating entrée to the Vatican, and I established a number of friends who were endlessly patient and generous, not the least of whom was Walter Persegati, then Secretary of the Vatican Museum.

Early in the work, when a potential publisher asked how many color plates the book would require, I replied, "None." I told him that I thought the book should be printed in black and white. I said, "We really do not know what color the frescoes are." I did not realize how prescient I was. I did know that the widely published pictures of the Sistine Ceiling in guidebooks and coffee table books were artificially produced, giving the frescoes a near comic-book quality. I also knew that the deep, mysterious brownish-yellow hues of the Sistine Ceiling, however cherished, were the result of layers of darkening varnishes and years of incense smoke, candle soot, water damage, and dirt.

Shortly after I began my work, in 1981 the Vatican announced that it would undertake the tremendous job of cleaning, repairing, and restoring the Sistine Ceiling. Extensive restoration of the fifteenth-century murals that line the chapel walls had already been completed with magnificent results.

This restoration and cleaning of the Sistine Ceiling was not its first. Through the centuries, several times the panels had been washed using primitive, unscientific methods and various layers of animal glue had been applied to brighten the colors. This time, teams of scientific restorers equipped with extensive equipment for chemical analysis, microscopic study, and computer imaging were to be employed. The world's attention was quickly focused on the Sistine Ceiling. Archives that had been buried for centuries were exhumed and being perused, and there were almost minute-by-minute reports on the restoration process.

Much attention was given to the kind of scaffolding that the restorers would use. Because it was anticipated that it would take at least a decade to complete the process, a prime consideration was to construct scaffolding that would allow visitors to visit the chapel during the restoration.

From the scant information available, it is known that Michelangelo rejected the scaffold that was offered to him by the Vatican architects and designed his own. Unfortunately, the details of that scaffolding were lost during the Sack of Rome in 1527; however, we did know that his scaffolding allowed for continuing use of the Sistine Chapel during the 4 years that Michelangelo painted the Ceiling.

The experts decided that the restoration work should move from the entrance to the altar wall. It was known that Michelangelo painted the Sistine Ceiling entrance to altar. After much study by a team of experts, it was decided that the best way to commence was to construct a horizontal bridge that moved on tracks supported above the cornice by the walls. It was to everyone's amazement that when the side walls were penetrated to secure the tracks, evidence was found that solved the long-standing mystery of Michelangelo's own design for the scaffolding. Working alone without a team of experts or a battery of computers, Michelangelo had come to the same conclusion regarding scaffold. His also was a moving horizontal bridge anchored above the cornice.

For me, initiation of the restoration project was a most

propitious event. In the frequent trips to Rome to visit the chapel for my research, I now had access to historical documents long buried in the Vatican archives. I also developed relationships with some of the restorers.

Although I was studying the entire composite of the Sistine Ceiling, I was especially fascinated by the last panel painted, the one directly above the altar, *Separation of Light from Darkness*. The panel is a swirl of action, boasting a curious hermaphrodism to the God form. He has breast formations. Surrounding the panel are the most androgynous of all his *ignudi* (male nude in Italian--the name generally given to the 20 seated male nudes that frame the central panels). In this panel, the most abstract of all the painting in the Sistine Ceiling, I saw the parthenogenetic dynamics of inspiration and creativity.

Separation of Light from Darkness was the last segment to be restored. You can image my excitement in 1988 when I was invited to climb on the scaffold to examine the panel.

A Visit with God

Evie and I arrived at the Vatican Museum at the appointed hour of the morning. We were quickly ushered through the crowds in the museum to the Pauline Chapel, the private chapel of the pope with its two later Michelangelo murals, *The Crucifixion of St. Peter* and

The Conversion of St. Paul. It was hard to pass quickly through such treasures, although we were promised a return visit later in the week. We entered the Sistine Chapel through a small door at mid-chapel.

The Chapel like always was packed with throngs as we elbowed our way toward the altar wall where a shaft from the scaffolding extended down to the floor. In the shaft was a birdcage-like elevator that barely held a restorer and the two of us. It quickly whisked us nonstop the 60 feet to the scaffolding platform.

The platform spanned the 44-foot width of the Chapel and was about 20 feet across with a very short railing on either side. It was filled with many tables on which sat computer screens, analytic equipment, and various drawing boards. There were about a dozen people studying, scrubbing, and painting. There was much activity on the platform, and a tremendous din rose from the crowd below.

Standing on the scaffold, we were about 2 feet below the frescos. I remembered a small sketch by Michelangelo that accompanied his poem about painting the Sistine Ceiling that resides in the Laurentian Library in Florence. In it he draws himself standing with craned neck, brush in hand, reaching up to paint the very piece I was now seeing. It was with no small effort that I resisted reaching up to touch what has become a sacred object.

We looked toward the entrance wall, 135 feet away. Through

the ages, the Sistine Ceiling has developed sags in many areas giving a strange undulation, almost a flowing to and fro, as one views the frescoes from eye level, so to speak. Because the restoration was nearly complete, we could see the blaze of pigments from deep purples to the subtlest of pastels of this gigantic mannerist painting. On the other side, we were adjacent to the altar wall's *Last Judgment,* which was completely covered for protection.

Examining the *Separation of Light from Darkness* was breathtaking. The impressionist quality intensified the etherealness of the God figure, and His pale purple cloak seemed to be flying. The swirl in the mist of creation was dizzying. God appeared at once near and distant.

As a demonstration of the cleaning process, one of the restorers took a sponge and wet it with distilled water. He made a wide slash on an untreated part of the ceiling and immediately the colors brightened. He rinsed the sponge in a pail of water, and the water blackened. There was little question that the Byzantine dimness was largely dirt and yellowed varnish.

I asked a restorer to show me some of Michelangelo's *secco* work. *Secco* is the watercolor tinting that fresco artists use to touch up the work after the fresco has dried. It is a way of correcting errors. We walked around a good deal before a bit could be found. I believe it was a finger nail. Clearly we could see that Michelangelo had applied a black line to change a form. The restorer and I looked at each other. With a grin, he said, "You know there really is very little *secco*." One could only think, "He did it right the first time." It was almost unbelievable to imagine how Michelangelo maintained the perspective of a viewer 70 feet below.

Evie and I were allowed to remain as long as we wanted, however, we could see that there was much work to be done and we were in the way. We walked over to the edge of the scaffold to look again toward the entrance wall. There, far below and indeed seeming very small, was a great mélange of colors, the huge throng of people from all over the world gathered to be inspired by this monumental achievement. Looking straight ahead across the ceiling lay the vast immensity of the colors coordinated into a celebration of humankind.

I thought of this nonheroic man whose work made visible the extraordinary power of the creative and integrative capacities of the mind, not to mention his Herculean physical effort. As I looked at Michelangelo's God in primal creation, I thought, "By creating *Creation*, Michelangelo was God incarnate." I was brought back to the temporal world when Evie leaned over and gently kissed me. "Thank you," she said. We both knew that we had had an experience of a lifetime.

A Crossing on the "Cue-Ee-Two"

(1995)

Lunch with Pat Steger was always an event. Her keen wit, enjoyment of salty jokes, vast knowledge of events, and intolerance for any sort of presumption made time with her fly by. Although she was San Francisco's leading social columnist and sought after by everyone, I enjoyed with her a near secret friendship based on our mutual appreciation of language and the foibles of humankind. For years, we would meet regularly for lunch, just the two of us. We always sat at an obscure table in an obscure restaurant where we would not be approached by people who recognized her and dropped information in the hopes that they would appear in her column.

It being late in 1994, Pat of course knew about the horrible year Evie and I had had with Evie's cancer. At the time, Evie was in a rare but sadly short remission when Pat, the master of cruises, suggested, "Why don't you two go on the 'cue-ee-two'?" It was some time before I translated "cue-ee-two" into the luxury steamship, the *Queen Elizabeth 2,* the then flagship of the Cunard Line.

I had always avoided the idea of a cruise, even though I

had spent hours hearing Pat's praise of many. Frankly, "cruise" sounded old, slow, and uninteresting. Nonetheless, I called Cunard, eventually mastering its complex telephone system. I managed to leave somewhere in the ether of voicemail my name, address, and a request for information. At that time at least, I must have been one of Cunard's few customers whose plans were not arranged by a travel agent.

One day an oversized envelope appeared. In it was a shiny brochure with a gorgeous picture of the magnificent ship profiled in a sunset-colored dreamy sea. The brochure profiled cruise after cruise and package after package, all beautifully colored and described, each making me less and less interested when without knowing it myself, I came upon what I was looking for--a transatlantic crossing.

The idea of a transatlantic crossing immediately conjured up boyhood memories of the Rialto Theater (pronounced "rye-all-tow-thee-aye-ter") in Rock Springs, Wyoming, watching the *Movietone News*. I could still picture the worthies of the world surrounded by mountains of luggage arriving in New York aboard castle-like vessels. I could hear the low-pitched steam whistle that always accompanied Douglas Fairbanks or the Duchess of Windsor as each spoke meaningless words of praise for the United States as the Statue of Liberty passed in the background. On a pragmatic level I thought the trip would not be physically taxing for Evie and would provide a much longed-for visit with our son, Noah, who lived in Paris and could meet us in London. Imagine arriving in Europe rested!

It was not my first time on a ship. The U.S. Navy provided me with 2 memorable years aboard ships, both large and small, in the Pacific during the early 1950s. I knew that I could never recapture the feeling of a 23-year-old lieutenant, junior grade, sailing into Yokohama Harbor. Nor will I forget my 1956 voyage to Europe on the Holland America Line with the amorphous plan to live in Europe as long as I could manage, which turned out to be 2 years. That 11-day passage on the Holland America ship, sharing a tiny stateroom with three others, is best forgotten. As hard as it is to believe, for that adventure, I carried less luggage and had much less money than I take today for 3 weeks in Europe.

It was not easy to understand the language of Cunard. First one had to learn that Cunard sells *class,* and it sells it subtly. With tutoring from Pat, I learned that Queen's Grill is first class, Princess/Britannia Grill is a major step below. An even larger step down is Caronia, called Deluxe. Deeply beneath is Mauretania, euphemistically called Premium. I could have saved much research had I just checked the fares. Coldly, prices tell one that high and forward are better.

It is a marvel of modern navigation that some 1,800 passengers and 1,000 crew can fit aboard one vessel. There are almost 1,000 passenger cabins honeycombed onto the eight decks devoted to cabins. One selects the cabin one wants; however, the color coding in the brochure is ever so subtle--mixing mauve with rose umber could be a disaster. The spaces allotted "Garage," "Laundromat," "Library," "The Pub," and "Harrods" make one wonder if it is a ship at all.

I was sure my choice of cabin would be critical, and I was equally sure this task would be best handled by an experienced travel agent. However, that is not my way. When it comes to selecting places to visit, hotels, and hotel rooms, I do it myself.

Common sense told me to stay away from the banks of thirteen elevators, the two theaters, the three dance floors, and the cinema. Yet, how was I to obtain the information from voicemail? In exasperation I left a message in the Cunard telephone limbo asking to speak to a person. To my surprise, my call was quickly returned by Brendan Vierra, Vice President of Sales and Service. Best of all, Mr. Vierra had his own fax (this being before e-mail). Thus began a lengthy electronic correspondence that I am sure Mr. Vierra was happy to conclude. Every question was answered promptly, down to what is the corkage charge in the dining room ($10.00). Dealing with Mr. Vierra evidenced that I had moved into a softer, gentler, and remarkable courteous world.

In the Cunard world, euphemisms prevail: Peak, Value, and Super Value--equate to expensive, less expensive, and cheapest. Evie and I began thinking we would go cheaply--in the minimal (Mauretania) accommodations off season. After all, we were not going to spend time in the cabin.

With increasing realization that the crossing is the event, we decided to go up a notch to the lowest level Queen's Grill, a subtle green in the brochure, in the shoulder season (value). However, our resolve for economy further foundered, I must add, imperiled by our battle with cancer and our increasingly acute awareness of our impermanence. Clearly we were becoming easy marks for Cunard's salesmanship; besides who can resist the "old shell game." We ended up booked during high season, Queen's Grill, complete with a terrace, and a return on the British Airways Concorde.

More literature, more decisions, a few forms later, and after numerous faxes to Mr. Vierra, we were all set. We were a little intimidated by a space on one form that asked for "Title." Evie uncharacteristically suggested that we put down "Professor."

Transport from the Southampton port to London seemed a major problem. The romantic sounding boat train had been discontinued and was replaced by buses. The idea of being loaded with 1,000 others onto buses after five days of sublimity was out of the question. Our London hotel offered to send a car but not a bank loan to cover the expense. Through a limousine service in San Francisco, we arranged for a Mercedes to meet us.

Our boat tickets arrived FedEx, even though there was ample time before we were to leave. Two luxurious wallets revealed two remarkably understandable tickets. The tickets simply read "Passage from New York to Southampton on the *Queen Elizabeth 2,* boarding between 1-3." A smaller wallet contained two tickets marked "British Airways, Concorde Flight #1" and the date. No need to hand over incomprehensible documents at a check-in counter hoping that one is using the right ticket to the right place. Tucked away in the great wallet were no less than eight black luggage tags stamped on one side with our name and cabin number; the other side stamped in gold read "Priority." Obviously the Queen's Grill was paying off.

With privilege came responsibility. Packing! A well-written, rather understated pamphlet of *Suggestions* noted that in the Queen's Grill, "Formal wear in keeping with the elegance of the ship is requested in the evening." Further reading revealed that "Formal wear is requested on only three of the five nights. On the first night when baggage is being sorted and stored and on the last night when best wear is packed, formal wear is not required." It did seem that every detail was being attended to and it did mean at least a tuxedo, two tux shirts, and special shoes for me and various long dresses, beaded jackets, gold shoes, stoles, and sequin pants for Evie. Suddenly it was clear why there were eight baggage tags. We began to long for the one fold-over-under-the-seat days.

How to get to the ship? Should we take the "red eye" and wander around New York before embarking in the afternoon to save a night's lodging in a hotel? Quickly, thoughts about money were set aside for reasons already noted. We chose a late afternoon flight to New York, a night at the Waldorf, a morning walk, and a leisurely brunch before the afternoon embarkation from the pier only blocks away. How civilized it was becoming. Why *do* we fly directly to Europe, which means that we arrive exhausted and ruin the first couple of days? It is easy to get caught up in modern time's emphasis on speed.

Arriving in New York late was a good idea. With the freeway clear and the skyline lighted, the 30-minute cab ride to the Waldorf Hotel was much more pleasant than watching the cabby struggle with bumper-to-bumper cars. Our hotel room was ready, although we arrived to a blinking light on the telephone. "Call Cunard in the morning!" was the ominous message.

Early the next day, we called. "The ship is delayed, but the damage is minimal," the Cunard woman reassured. Later, we learned that the ship had been caught in a hurricane. British understatement can be infuriating.

A day's delay meant an unplanned but not unwelcome day and night in New York. Cunard offered to offset our expenses, however, its idea of what an extra day and night in New York costs and reality are, to say the least, different. After many calls we learned that we could embark after 4:00 p.m. the next day with a midnight departure scheduled.

The cab ride to the New York Passenger Terminal on the Hudson River was mercifully short. The terminal was cavernous and very quiet. A porter met the cab and told us that the bags would be in our cabin in less than a half hour. After his third reassurance, I realized that a tip in advance was expected. We walked into a giant balloon-bedecked empty space. Not a soul was to be seen. It looked like the night after a ball. At the far end was a lone ancient man in a blue uniform, whom we approached. He checked our ticket, forgetting to give us boarding passes, and wished us a good voyage. All was calm and unhurried, and light years away from an airport. With no one there, there was an unspoken, awesome concern that everybody knew something that we did not.

The covered gangway, so long and broad that it scarcely

seemed a gangway, led to a huge art deco central lounge, well upholstered and trimmed in polished brass and mahogany. We were not sure if we were yet on the ship. With hesitation we ventured further. A large brightly polished brass plaque noted decks and rooms "fore and aft." We found a bank of elevators and pressed the top button hoping for the best.

We exited the elevator and found many stewards in white, freshly pressed, double-breasted jackets with gold buttons and gold and black epaulets giving unhurried, warm greetings with difficult-to-understand Irish, Scottish, and North Country accents. It was hard to keep in mind that they had as much difficulty understanding us as we, them. Unconsciously we clipped our speech somewhat hoping to be better understood and seem more sophisticated.

More wrong turns and more elevators led to our being delivered to Peter, a Scot with flaming red hair and a delightful and at times dour attitude, who introduced himself as our butler. He in turn introduced Joanne, with equally flaming red hair, as our maid. We felt very much in first class as they escorted us to our cabin and asked to assist us in any way they could.

The cabin was spacious with huge closets, a queen bed, a large television that we never learned how to use, and a small refrigerator. The outside wall was three floor-to-ceiling windows that opened onto a small terrace and the skyline of New York beyond. The marble bathroom with tub and shower had ample shelves, tabletop space, and cabinets.

Shortly, our bags arrived via different men from the ones on the dock and required yet more tips. Peter and Joanne unpacked us, asking about where to place various items. They then removed our bags. With the midnight departure, we were invited to have dinner on board although the ship was operating a shuttle to mid-town Manhattan should we want to have dinner in New York.

As we moved about the ship, rumors began to mount. The ship had been delayed because it had been hit by a 95-foot wave. Peter confessed that "it was a bit rough." On both sides, I think humor disguised anxiety.

Being late afternoon, we explored the ship and got lost at every turn. Easily one loses any sense of forward and aft, port and starboard. Everywhere, the ship with its art deco flourishes sparkled from the recent refurbishment. Few were aboard, and the ship seemed like an out-of-season, staid, resort hotel that was managing to hang on to its dignity despite encroaching anachronism.

Dinner in port was "informal," which meant dark jacket and tie. The food was also a colossal disappointment. Our cordial, spirited young waiter, a Yorkshire lad who asked to be called Andy, too many times asked if everything were all right. After the third, "How is everything?" I told him I was sure the sturgeon was frozen and badly prepared. My candor resulted in a prompt visit from the table captain, Raoul, who apologized and explained that I should have called him immediately. He assured us that in the future he would personally take our orders, adding that we could order anything we wanted at any time. That proved to be nearly literally true.

After dinner, we gathered on the decks for a balmy good-bye to New York. At the stroke of midnight, the water churned behind unseen tugs and the nose of the giantess slowly edged away from the dock, turning into the Hudson. The hotel became a ship. The lighted skyline with its monuments to immigrant success and their reflections in the water were beautiful and exciting.

We felt obliged to see the Statue of Liberty. As mist softened New York, suddenly Evie exclaimed, "I think I see it." The orange torch glowed and "it" became a Greek goddess welcoming and bidding farewell. The obligatory tourist event brought unashamed tears. The greenish glow of liberty, not the bright lights of wealth, became a poignant allegory of our national identity.

We slept wonderfully. As prearranged with Peter, we awoke the next morning to his bringing us morning tea and opening the drapes. That was our first view of the open sea. Five brisk laps walking around the boat deck, 1 mile, was followed by breakfast. The miserable dinner was redeemed by the excellent scrambled eggs aside a huge mound of fresh osetra caviar and crème fraîche. A steward informed us that we were invited to the visit the bridge and have coffee with the captain and his wife. We were discreetly told that it would be just the four of us.

The bridge was reached by stairs somewhat above the signal deck where our cabin was. It felt like it was out of a starship, eerily silent and serene. Two officers were on watch, looking crisp in their white uniforms. With soft voices they demonstrated the elaborate electronic tracking devices and the tiny wheel now working on autopilot that guided the great ship. However, the real fascination was with the gigantic bow, endlessly plunging into the sapphire sea ahead.

Noon was approaching, and the first officer asked which of us would like to blow the ship's whistle. Evie was easily, though reluctantly, elected. At their command she pressed the large button for three short blasts and one long one. We were told that the whistle, a deep bass, could be heard for a radius of 8 miles. Evie looked triumphant.

On the bridge that first morning, with no turning back, we learned the full story of the delay in the arrival and the departure.

Two days out from New York, the vessel had been hit by the largest wave that had ever hit the *QE2*. Although the bridge is 95 feet above the water line, the wave washed over it. One of the officers who had been on the bridge that night described, "It was a clear night and the sea was very rough. We were proceeding at 5 knots. We saw this huge wave moving toward us like a mountain. Fearing that the windshields of the bridge would not withstand the assault, we ducked as it crashed over us. The radar scanner on the mast above the bridge was hit and torn loose." The officer, in his understated way, too many times said, "She was built to take it."

From the bridge we could see clearly that the fo'c'sle was buckled and the railing hastily repaired. By coincidence, we were on the bridge at the very point eastward at which the ship was hit as it traveled westward.

We left the bridge by way of a short stairwell down that opened into the spacious and homey Captain's Quarters where we were greeted by Captain Ronald Warwick. Captain Warwick, age 54, was slim with a full and trimmed white beard, blue eyes, and leathery skin. He succeeded his father as captain of the *QE2*. He introduced his lovely and lively young Hawaiian wife, Kim, who always sailed with him. While Kim served coffee, we talked of ships, crossings, and cruises. We shared memories of sailing under the Golden Gate

Bridge and the beauty of San Francisco. Mostly, we talked of their love of the ship. There were numerous interrupting telephone calls from various newspapers. Obviously the wave was a big event and Cunard was doing its best to underplay it. Over and over we heard, "A lesser ship would have been severely damaged." The time alone with the captain and his wife added much to our trip. When we saw them at the numerous parties to which we were later invited, they seemed like old friends.

On the ship there was always much talk about food. Eating centered the day. We had asked that attention be given to Evie's need for low-fat, low-cholesterol food. We had not anticipated how much attention that would receive, which could not have been more in a hospital or at a spa.

All of the dining rooms had open hours, and in some ways the Princess and Britannia Grills were more intimate than the Queen's Grill, although I did not see many tables for two. The captain always ate in the Princess Grill. We never visited the midnight buffet in the Lido, the aft night club.

The food in general was good to somewhat better than good. The service was attentive and youthful. It did not quite have the professional reserve that the setting and style require, but in general the meals were well served considering that the Queen's Grill seats nearly 240 passengers.

The Queen's Grill is over-lighted, which seemed to encourage talking between tables. From what we could overhear, these conversations were far from stimulating. Our table for two was somewhat distant from nearby tables and by a window. Our location turned out to be excellent. Better to be short of conversation, which we never were, than to wish there were no conversation.

Each morning Raoul, the table captain, came to our cabin as he indicated he would after our first unhappy dinner to present the menu for the day. He reiterated, "You can order anything that you want prepared any way you want." We felt that we had finally conquered the dining room. When asked about selections, Raoul carefully mentioned which were of necessity frozen, a reference to our first meal aboard. Pleasantly he added, "Fowl freezes better than fish."

It was an extraordinary experience to realize that we literally could create the dinner that we wanted. It was also somewhat daunting. On and off the menus, the fancy touches were there: fresh caviar, sautéed fresh foie gras, lobster, soufflés, venison, and game birds. And yet at heart the food was best when we stayed with dishes of high style and classical preparation. We found the duck à l'orange, sautéed fresh foie gras, and the venison chateaubriand, none of which appeared on the menu, to be the best. Raoul's crêpes suzettes, again not on the menu, were among the best we had ever had, even in France.

I was told that it takes 55 pounds of caviar to carry the ship from New York to Southampton. The freshness and quality was high. Evie accused me of eating most of those 55 pounds.

On the third day out, a knock on the door in the morning unexpectedly revealed a young steward with a small envelope on a silver plate. A note indicated that the captain would be pleased if we would host a small cocktail party in our stateroom on his behalf for the Earl and Countess of Iddesleigh. The note suggested that the party be at 8:00 p.m. We were dumbfounded, but we indicated that it would be our pleasure.

At 7:45 p.m., again a knock. Outside were several young waiters and a trolley of hors-d'oeuvres with several buckets with champagne. Expertly the waiters rearranged our sitting room, and one remained to serve. At 8:00 p.m., the earl and countess arrived. They were a delightful couple. He talked about dinner and said that he had ordered grouse "to test the kitchen." Realizing that that was an excellent idea, I asked the waiter if that were possible for me. The answer was a polite "Of course."

Lord and Lady Iddesleigh talked much about shooting, their home in Devon, and some talk about the storm that we were all glad to have missed. The countess told some amusing stories about being titled and traveling in the United States. "They always think his first name is Earl," she chuckled. The earl added, "They say, 'Hi, Earl, do you want a beer?'"

The four of us went for dinner and we suffered through the earl's complaining about the grouse that I, on the other hand, thoroughly enjoyed. "None of the delicious heather flavor," the earl groused.

The following evening, we met the earl and countess for drinks. We exchanged addresses, but we knew that this was a formality of travel. We were aware that we would probably never see one another again. To this day I wonder why we were chosen to be their hosts. Was it the good work of Mr. Vierra making sure that we enjoyed our crossing? Had the Captain been looking us over to see if we were interesting people to entertain some of the more distinguished guests? Or did someone know Pat Steger and know that she had encouraged our trip? The truth remains a mystery and an enjoyable serendipity.

On returning to our cabin, under the door was an engraved invitation to a small cocktail party in the Captain's Cabin the next evening. The party was crowded and congenial. However, it did give us an opportunity to chat again with the Iddeslieghs. We began to wonder who Cunard thought we were.

Dancing after dinner was a nice touch, however, in general we found the ship's evening entertainment best avoided. The musical reviews in the main theater included a violinist playing "Dear Dark Eyes That Shine" and Brahms's "Hungarian Dance No. 5." The people next to us thought it wonderful, "almost as good as *Miss Saigon*." The next day a lecture on Buckingham Palace was a series of inane anecdotes illustrating how human the royal family is. Although much is made of the activities, we found them of little interest. The Computer Learning Center essentially sold electronic products, and the shops are at airport level. The *QE2* souvenirs are close to San Francisco's Fisherman's Wharf ware. The art lessons, dancing lessons, scarf tying class, and deck sports were well attended but seemed forced.

The swimming pool is aft, a one block walk that required the use of several elevators, but was a lot of fun. The warm sea water jostled and sloshed about as the ship drove through the waves below. The pool is small and uncomfortable with more than four people in it. Fortunately it was always empty before breakfast and after tea.

For those of us who cannot believe Las Vegas, the casino with its lines of electronic slot machines being cranked by elderly women also could not be believed, especially at 10:00 a.m. With a drink in one hand and a cigarette in the other, the coordination of sip, puff, and pull was remarkable to watch. How glad we were that these players rarely ventured beyond the casino's walls for the length of the voyage. At night, however, when most of the men wore black tie and the tables were operating, there was a certain James Bond glamour to the scene.

Deep and mid-ships was a spa with a very small indoor pool. I cannot imagine why. On a visit, I saw platoons of men and women on exercise machines pumping and groaning. I do not think that they were actually powering the ship, but they looked like galley slaves on their benches, deep in the bowels of the ship pulling and pushing giant oars.

On the whole, the passengers in Queen's Grill were much younger than we anticipated. The kyphotic and the caned, the old people, seemed to be largely below. Among our "class," we did find our share of writers, T.V. producers, and many Americans who had made huge amounts of money in surprisingly banal ways. Most have traveled extensively, but generally with tours or on cruises. We learned quickly not to discuss fares. Everyone had a deal. We soon felt that ours was the most expensive fare on board. Even Countess Iddesleigh had a deal.

We did venture into other "classes." Travel-wise, the Princess

Grill had much to recommend it. The cabins were large with large oval-shaped portholes that could be opened with a sense of nearness to the sea. If one were young and wanted to do it on the cheap, Caronia (Decks 2 and 3) is better than passable. One would have to be a student or a dedicated Spartan to travel Mauretania, especially inside on Decks 4 and 5.

On the fourth night, we were invited to the Wardroom Officers' party. It was "jolly good fun." The wardroom looked like a combination of pub and London club. It was decorated with old mahogany and polished brass, with many mementos of war and distinguished activities and visitors. It strongly reminded me of my days on a Royal Navy frigate. The officers wore short formal white jackets with gold buttons and their rank on black and gold epaulets. Everyone looked wonderful, especially Kim, the captain's wife, in her sleek, sequined dress.

The officers drank a lot. I hoped the "watch" was not there, and I worried about the next day--like I often did when I was assigned to the Royal Navy.

At these parties, officers and passengers began to look familiar and we realized that, like at home in San Francisco, there are those who are invited to and attend every party. I never found out the secret of the selection, particularly ours.

We occasionally enjoyed our terrace. An unexpected advantage of a terrace cabin was that the windows were washed daily, something impossible on the lower levels. After even one day at sea, the windows of the "less privileged" were hard to see though and were almost opaque by voyage end.

The weather was lovely, growing grayer as we traveled north. The seas were always quiet; the wind and spray, a welcome constant reminder that we were at sea in the North Atlantic. The skies were largely opalescent; the water, a cool gray occasionally frosted with white caps and churned turquoise by the ship's screws. On bright moments, the sea reached a sapphire blue. It was the limitlessness of the sea's passing that was both lulling and at times curiously dispiriting. The misty horizon would close in and open up, but always it was only the touch of sky on sea. At times we were treated to God's own lamé as the sun reflected off the following sea, largely silver, sometimes richly reddened by the setting sun. The sea was the great reward of the voyage.

As we approached England, the weather misted over. On the last day, we received bulletins concerning arrival time and procedures. We were told that on a lower deck Her Majesty's Customs Officer would assist. There never was a line, and we enjoyed the privilege of going leisurely through customs. Although Her Majesty's Customs

Officer looked like ship's personnel, the way he courteously said, "How long will you be in England?" and the way he stamped our passports revealed a bureaucratic legacy.

Because of the delays, we were informed that the ship would arrive at Southampton at 6:00 a.m. on the sixth day. We were at liberty to leave the ship any time after 7:00 a.m. The evening before disembarking, our bags reappeared, and lovely Joanne with her red hair repacked us. The bags were miraculously removed by unseen hands.

On our last morning, at 6:45 a.m. as requested, Peter arrived with morning tea, and we leisurely showered and dressed for London. The ship silently slid next to the dock. We had breakfast, said our good-byes, were presented with menus by the dining room staff, and left our envelopes of gratuities. Cunard's own suggestions seemed a little on the meager side. We added to the suggested amounts for Andy, Joanne, Peter, Raoul, and the wine steward, knowing that they would not reach them individually but mentioning them by name.

At 8:30 a.m., we walked comfortably and somewhat sadly down the gangway, where our driver in full uniform was waiting. Our bags were in a line, and the driver drove the car to the bags. In minutes we were on our way--fresh, rested, and ready for London.

To say the least, the crossing more than fulfilled our hopes and fantasies. We did not want it to end. Would we do it again? I am not sure, but I am glad that we did. I was prescient in fearing that a crossing on such a ship would not be possible much longer, likewise, about the Concorde. Our experience was a race against anachronism, and I think we won. As I read about the *QE2's* successor, the *Queen Mary 2,* I fear it may be a disappointment--even more a floating resort oriented within itself and less a ship oriented toward the sea. Even though Evie and I thoroughly enjoyed the restfulness, the elegance, and the gracefulness of the ship and crew, the enduring memory is of the sea.

A Word About Our Return

Our Queen's Grill passage included return on the ship, a flight from London to New York on the British Airways Concorde, or a first-class seat on the nonstop London-San Francisco British Airways flight. We chose the Concorde for the experience. What a mistake. The British Concorde, with its indifferent service, broken promises, and lackluster food was nothing more than a quick, uncomfortable shuttle from London to New York, and a far cry from the *QE2.* If one wants to experience the Concorde, take the Air France Concorde--first-class in the best sense of the word.

Postscript

Of course Evie and I knew but scarcely uttered that this was our penultimate adventure. Our ultimate adventure together, short and wretched, followed as she soon was relentlessly ravaged by her disease. Relief only came when she disappeared into death.

Sinan's Hammam

(1997)

My first visit to Istanbul, Turkey, was with Evie in 1966.
We had taken the antiquated, much romanticized Simplon Orient
Express from Ankara to Üsküdar. Although the train was a little
shabby, it was still filled with mystery and charm. The red velvet seats
were worn smooth, but at night the ancient porters made them into
comfy beds.

The train arrived in Constantine's ancient capital at day
break and met the ferry crossing the Bosporus from Asia to Europe.
No sight compares with approaching Istanbul at dawn by water
from Asia. We were greeted by the sun just topping the domes and
minarets making an incredible profile and the *muezzins* calling from
all directions. Istanbul quickly fulfilled my fantasy by combining
adventure with exoticism. I knew that I would visit again.

Thirty years later, flying into Istanbul was less dramatic, but
my anticipation was great. I now knew much more about the ever-
complex Middle East, and I was excited to explore the city in which
much excavation and restoration had taken place since my first visit.

The Man in Nagasaki

I was quickly rewarded when I checked into the beautiful Four Seasons Hotel, only steps from the Hagia Sophia, one of Instanbul's most precious gifts to humanity. How fortunate I was in that the hotel gave me one of its few rooms with a view of the Sea of Mamara. I was in bliss.

There were many sights to revisit and many new to explore. On this visit, I had more time for the museums and small mosques, and I wanted unhurried visits to the Sultanahmet Camii, the ever-graceful Blue Mosque, and Sinan's Suleymaniye Camii, the Mosque of Suleyman.

As I entered the Blue Mosque, I could not help but be amused by my memory of the visit in 1966. At that time, visitors were allowed into the mosque only between times of prayer, and then like now, one was required to remove one's shoes upon entering. Men and women did not enter or sit together, so Evie and I went through separate entrances and were in separate sections.

On entering the vast central space, I was soon on my hands and knees setting up my Exakta camera on its small tripod and peering into the top of the camera's ground glass screen. Deeply engaged in photographing the vastness, the beautiful blue windows, the calligraphy, and the marvelous tiles, suddenly I realized that I was surrounded by other kneeling men. In my intense concentration, I had not noticed that the mosque had been cleared of visitors and the faithful let into pray. Kneeling over my camera, I had been mistaken for a believer deep in prayer. When I realized I was in the midst of the prayers, all I could do was to try to follow what the fellow next to me was doing and hope that I would not be detected. Meanwhile Evie was waiting outside for me, both fearful and upset with my dalliance.

In preparing for the second visit, I had become especially interested in Sinan (1489-1588), the most highly revered Ottoman architect. At the Suleymaniye Camii, I was told that Sinan had designed a *hammam* (bath) in Istanbul. I was determined to find it.

The next day, I set out on foot asking directions as I went. Easily every man I asked knew what and where it was. Yet, I made several wrong turns. Finally a young man who was pleased that I knew about the bath offered to lead me there. I learned that the actual name of the bath was Cemberlitas Hammami, but everyone called it Sinan's Hammam.

My new friend and I wound our way through the many tiny streets of the oldest part of the city near the Kprl Mohmud Pasa complex of schools, mosques, and tombs and near the Kapali Carsisi (Grand Bazaar). Finally, we arrived at a door in front of which sat two men smoking a *nargile* (oriental water pipe). Neither man looked up as we approached.

I had wanted to see the architecture of the hammam, but
the buildings were so tightly placed and the streets so narrow that
I could see nothing of Sinan's building. I walked through the very
dilapidated entrance, all the while doubting the wisdom of this
adventure. I came to a desk of sorts behind which was a wall, much
marred by age and peeling plaster, on which was painted in Turkish a
list of items and amounts.

A young man who spoke little English appeared, and I told
him as best I could that I wanted to see the building. I quickly got
the idea that the only way to see it was to have a bath. The man
pointed to the sign behind the desk and said something that sounded
like "Sultan's treatment." I assumed that meant "the full treatment."
Unsure of the cost, I nodded and handed him some Turkish notes.
He gave me change. I felt somewhat reassured that he was not about
to take advantage of me.

The young man led me to a room that was divided into
a series of small cubicles, each with a cot. He gave me a basket
with a lock on it, a *pestemal* (small printed cotton wrap), and some
wooden clogs. He motioned that I should undress. I had taken the
precaution of leaving in the hotel my valuables, save my watch. I was
reluctant to leave my belongings, especially the watch, but I knew

that the whole excursion would have been in vain if I did not forge ahead.

I undressed, put everything in the basket, and wrapped the pestemal around me like a kilt. When I stepped out of the cubicle, the same young man, now wearing clogs and a similar kilt, was waiting.

He motioned me to follow him through a warm, dank, dark corridor in which water seemed to drip from every pore. We entered a large steam-filled 10-sided polygonal-shaped room, *the sicaklek,* that was capped by a dome. Perhaps 40 feet high, the dome was pierced by randomly placed squares of thick clear glass. Sunlight streamed in through the glass squares, and in the dense steam became beacons of light.

A huge, 10-sided slab of marble, the *gobek tasi,* occupied much of the center of the room. This enormous platform was about 3 feet off the floor and slightly canted toward the center. On its periphery lay several men, some being "worked on" by attendants; some lying quietly in the steam.

Like the gobek tasi, the walls of the polygonal room were marble, and each side of the polygon contained a niche, about 4 feet deep and 6 feet wide. Framed by columns, a marble pointed arch created an entry way into each niche. On the back wall of each was a lion-headed marble wall fountain that was about 5 feet off the floor. These fountains spouted a full force of water that dropped into carved marble basins that indented the floor.

The sicaklek was heated by a fire below the giant marble slab. The room was warm, but not hot like a sauna, and silent except for the sounds of the fountains. The steamy atmosphere combined with the intensely penetrating beams of light playing on the carved marble surfaces and the near naked men moving silently made it seem other worldly.

The young man motioned for me to lie prone on the warm slab, and he began the massage. It was a kneading process that started deep in the arches of my feet and worked upwards with much stretching of limbs and joints. As he leaned over me, I could feel his sweat dripping from his body mixing with mine as natural oil for the massage. His deep massage became increasingly vigorous, and before long my kilt was somewhere off the side of my head and I could see his lying on the floor.

I have no idea how long he worked with me prone, but at a point he motioned for me to turn over. I thought, "Please, I need a spatula!" Never have I felt such utter relaxation. With much help, I rolled over. I noticed that the young man had replaced his kilt and held mine in such a way as to preserve my privacy. Islamic men are markedly modest. He next began his magical work on my front. Again the process was a deep kneading, spending much time on my neck and scalp.

To my surprise, the man produced a bucket of warm water overflowing with suds. Using a strange piece of toweling, somewhat like a wash cloth with several short tails, he dipped the cloth in the suds and began a shampoo that slowly progressed downward. He placed the sponge under my kilt, and in a sensual but not sexual way he washed these areas.

When I was completely encased with billowing thick suds, he motioned me to stand. I could barely move, but I managed to stagger after him into one of the lion fountain niches. With a huge pail the man took warm water from the fountain and poured it vigorously over me.

Dripping wet, he led me back to my small cubicle. He handed me several large towels, and he returned the basket of my items. He indicated that I could lie on the cot as long as I wished, but it looked rather unkempt and I declined. I did not want to spoil the freshness that I felt. I do not think I have felt that scrubbed since my mother bathed me when I was a baby.

I dressed and was pleased to find my watch still in the basket. Back at the desk, the young man, now dressed in long, black pants but no shirt, was waiting. I gave him the expected tip, and he thanked me in the overly courteous manner of Turkish men.

When I walked out into the bright sunlight, I was delighted to be in the old part of the city. I walked slowly back to my hotel, so that the centuries only gradually turned ahead. Regrettably, I was never able to see the exterior of Sinan's Hammam, however, I felt a part of it.

Marley and the Duchess

(1999)

Although it is always a pleasure to visit Elizabeth, the
Duchess of Manchester, in her home in London or in her beautiful
cottage on the 17 Mile Drive in Carmel, California, there is no
treat like visiting her in her palazzo in Venice. To my mind, the
graceful Palazzo Vendramin is the most beautifully restored and most
perfectly situated palazzo in Venice. On the Giudecca, its *piano
nobile* (principal floor) with its row of Venetian tracery and gothic
pointed windows faces directly across the canal into the Piazza San
Marco. The windows frame the Basilica San Marco and the Torre
dell'Orologio with its two giant moors. To one side sits the Dogana
di Mare and the dome-like towers of the Santa Maria della Salute on
the Dorsodura, the entrance to the Grand Canal, and the Libreria
Sansonviana on the main island. On the other side is the Palazzo
Ducale.

Elizabeth, the widow of the Duke of Manchester, is an elegant
woman with creamy skin, snow white hair, a graceful petite carriage,
and a rare wit. Her softly flowing pastel dresses are generally accented

by large pearls and a startling diamond ring. Her conversation is strikingly free of pretension and yet reflects the extraordinary life she has lived and the extraordinary people who were and are her friends. The palazzo, like her other homes, is richly furnished in antiques and valuable art and objects. It is sheer serendipity that I know her and am frequently able to visit her.

I often arrange a visit with Elizabeth when she and I are both in Venice where I keep a small apartment on the Campo Santa Maria del Giglio near the Gritti Palace Hotel. I was particularly pleased one year when my elder daughter, Cici, and my granddaughter Marley, then age 10, were to stay with me during a time when Elizabeth was in Venice.

Before my family arrived, I had had lunch with Elizabeth at the Hotel Cipriani, and I mentioned Cici and Marley's visit. Graciously, Elizabeth said, "Jerry would you like them to come to the palazzo?" She followed the invitation with, "Why don't they come for tea on Friday?"

Friday came, and both Cici and Marley were excited to meet the duchess and see the palazzo. While riding in the boat to the palazzo, Marley asked "Granddaddy, what do I call her?" I thought her question perceptive. "I call her Elizabeth, but you should call her 'Duchess,'" I answered. I went on to say, "You should use her title in addressing her a little more than you would when you speak ordinarily. What I mean is that you say, 'How do you do, Duchess?' Not just 'How do you do?' If she asks if you want something, you should answer, 'Yes, thank you, Duchess,' rather than just 'Yes, thank you.'"

Marley was clearly intrigued and said, "Do I curtsy when I meet her?" I was surprised that she even knew about curtsies. I said, "No, but when she comes into the room, I will go over to kiss her, and it would be nice if you stood."

We arrived at the palazzo and were shown into the richly furnished living room. Before long Elizabeth came in, and I went over to kiss her and to introduce Marley and Cici. Both stood as I suggested. Elizabeth extended her hand to Marley and said, "I am pleased to meet you." Marley responded, "I am pleased to meet you, Duchess." Elizabeth asked, "Marley, would you like tea or do you prefer a Coke?" Marley answered, "I would like a Coke, Duchess."

Our tea together was delightful, and I was proud of my little granddaughter. Soon it was time to leave. At the door, Elizabeth said to Marley, "I hope you will come again, Marley." Marley, said, "I would be very pleased to, Duchess." Then we left.

We walked down to the waiting boat to take us back to my apartment. Marley was strangely silent. After a while she said,

"Granddaddy, how did she become a duchess?" I answered, "Well, Marley, she married a duke."

Again a long silence, and then Marley looked up and said, "Granddaddy, are there any more dukes around?"

The Dove

(1999)

It was a short drive from Mandalay to the Sagaing hills. In Burma (Myanmar) even short distances bring a great deal. Every turn of the road was graced by the view of golden stupas and idyllic-looking agrarian activities. Evening was approaching, and I was treated to processions of straight-backed, saffron-robed young monks, heads shaven, graciously collecting offerings for the monasteries and temples from poor, pious farmers and villagers.

Sagaing, an ancient capital, is one of many pagoda sites in the hills southwest of Mandalay. Luck took me to a beautiful, pure white marble temple--a glistening platform surrounding a tall, gold-plated stupa with pavilions housing various images of Buddha and ceremonial bells. The temple's platform juts out with a full view of the winding Irrawaddy River and the valley extending east across the Shan Plateau to China.

I arrived at sunset, and the complex was ablaze with pink, rose, and red and the sparking gleam of the golden stupa. I was one of the few people there. I removed my sandals and walked barefoot on the sun-warmed marble. I was thankful for the silence only occasionally penetrated by the deep gong of a temple bell as a devotee called forth divine attention before praying. Largely, all I heard was the soft shuffle of a few other bare feet and the soft tinkle of the *hti,* the gold-plated decorative umbrella topping the stupa.

I perched myself on the platform's edge transfixed by the magnificent vista. The brown Irrawaddy had turned pink, and the sky glowed with a million minute flaming particles that make sunsets in the Orient beyond words.

Lost in my thoughts that were heavily laced with an imperceptible sadness, I sensed a presence. Silently, a huddled, tiny, pink form, a nun, had moved discretely beside me. She looked into my face and I into hers, her face made more pure by shaven hair, large almond-shaped eyes, and the gentle caress of her pink robe. I thought of Evie rendered bald by the ravages of chemotherapy.

The nun held out her hands. At first I thought she was asking for a coin, and I reached into my pocket. She shook her head "no," and I realized that her hands were cupped rather than open. By motions, she indicated that I should do the same, and I extended cupped hands toward her. She reached beneath her robe, brought out a dove, and placed it in my hands.

The dove was warm, soft, and trembling. I was seized by

the wretched yet poignant memory of holding Evie--her beautiful body hacked to pieces by cancer and surgery as the silence of death progressed.

After a moment, the nun lifted her cupped hands and parted them. I knew that I was to do the same, releasing the quivering bird. The bird took immediate flight over the Irrawaddy. Effortlessly soaring and flapping her wings, she flew into a limitless horizon. Timelessly, she said good-bye.

My eyes filled with tears, and I looked down. My silent companion in this ritual of release had left me alone.

A Dance in Burma

(1999)

After two weeks of travel in northern Burma (Myanmar), I returned to Yangon for a stay in the Strand Hotel. I have an uncontrollable desire to enjoy famous old hotels. Even though I approach each with hesitation, I am rarely disappointed. The Strand's association with Rudyard Kipling and Somerset Maugham made it compelling. Built in 1898 by the Raffles group from Singapore, I had read that the hotel had recently been carefully restored. I was determined to stay there even though it is in a less attractive part of Yangon than the beautiful Pansea where I stayed on my way North.

The Strand is located deep in the heart of the commercial and trading center of old Yangon on the Yangon River. The area is busy with old-fashioned cargo loading docks and jetties. The building is an imposing square with a frontal colonnade. The large Colonial-style lobby is replete with immaculately and colorfully uniformed doormen and footmen.

Upon entry, I was greeted by the manager, a young woman from New Zealand. When I asked for my room key, I was told that there was no need for a key because my houseboy-butler would accompany me to my room. The houseboy wore the traditional Burmese jacket and *longyi* (the skirt-like sarong pulled up between the legs) and led the way to my huge suite overlooking the river. He or his replacement sat on a small stool in front of my door 24 hours a day, eager to do my bidding. Meticulous and silent, he entered and straightened out whatever I left behind as I moved from room to room. Whenever I left the suite, the elevator was always waiting for me. It was almost too much when he would press the proper floor number in the automatic elevator so that I would not have to attend to such matters. Clearly the Strand was a hotel from a different era. Once again, my adventurous spirit, at least regarding hotels, had not failed me.

I was excited to be able to revisit the magnificent Shwedagon Pagoda, which I had already carefully investigated earlier on my trip. The temple is the most important religious site in Yangon and, indeed, perhaps in all Myanmar, as it links Myanmar to the origins of Buddhism in Southeast Asia. Legend has it that two Burmese brothers, traders, converted to Buddhism by Guatama while journeying abroad. They returned home, carrying several hairs from Guatama's head. With these relics, they brought Buddhism to Myanmar. The eleventh-century Shwedagon Pagoda was built over the sacred relics. Of all the temples and shrines I have visited anywhere in the world, none rivals the Shwedagon for magnificent and extensive gold plating and gold leafing.

Located centrally in Yangon, the temple was not far from the Strand. Eagerly I remounted the stairs up the 50-foot retaining walls to the acres of marble that formed the main terrace of the temple. Among the morass of pagodas, stupas, shrines, bells, and pavilions centered on the main terrace was the main stupa. Its circumference exceeded 4 football fields. Rising above the terrace were a series of lesser terraces at first rectangular and then octagonal, leading to the bell of the stupa nearly 6 stories high. The bell itself rises to a foot turban topped by an inverted bow and a slender spire that holds a gigantic weather vane. I was told that atop the weather vane rested a 76-carat diamond. Incredibly, this entire vast expanse of religious consecration, rising a dizzying 14 stories, was covered not by gold gilt but by plates of gold.

I arrived at the temple in the late afternoon as the lowering sun cast long shadows on the throngs, a constant feature of this great complex, and reddened the dazzling marble and gold of the Shwedagon. How fortunate I was to come upon a gold raising ceremony at the main stupa.

In rich deep red and bright saffron robes, priests moved

among fifteen or more groups of villagers, each group in colorful native outfits typical of its village. Mostly in families, the devotees sat cross-legged on the temple platform chanting barely audibly as great horns, conches, and gongs rhythmically sounded. With the blast from a conch, a village leader arose and proudly brought forth a plate of solid gold, perhaps 6 feet square, festooned with ribbons and ornaments, and handed it to a priest. The plate was then ceremoniously attached to a cable that rose to the peak of the stupa. At the sound of the conch, the chanting increased and the clang of gongs, drums, and horns reached a cacophony of brilliance as the plate rapidly rose to a great height on the stupa. Received by half naked men in white loin clothes, the plate was attached in place and the conch blown again. An elder from another village then rose to present the priests with the gold plate from his village. The process repeated with great solemnity as each village in turn added to the brilliance of the great stupa. Clearly each plate represented years of sacrifice and devotion.

On returning to the hotel, I confessed to my ever-patient guide, Win Myint, who had traveled with me all over Myanmar, that I longed to see a traditional dance concert before I left his wonderful country. Earlier in my visit, I had arranged to see a supposedly traditional performance in a hotel in Mandalay that was less than satisfying. Clearly a tourist affair, it was a highly puffed up performance designed, unsuccessfully, to keep Japanese businessmen, who traveled in Myanmar in great abundance, awake. I saw enough to know that I had not seen what I wanted and enough to know that I wanted to see more. Win promised to check.

A few hours later Win returned to the hotel saying, "Professor, there is a concert at one of the hotels. I do not think you will like it. It is for visitors." By this time, I knew that "visitors" was his euphemism for Japanese businessmen, who often were drunk. He added shyly, "I know of a concert for us." He meant for Burmese people. "It is not in a fancy place, but I think it is for you." I responded, "Win, you've always given me good advice. I would like to do it."

At the appointed time, a car arrived and whisked me through narrow and dark streets to a relatively dilapidated, 1920s building lighted on the outside by a few bare bulbs. Undaunted, I entered into a moderately large auditorium that looked like it also served as a basketball court. At one end was a full stage with equipment for lighting and to the side a richly ornamented boat-like structure holding the characteristic collection of gongs, drums, and various percussion instruments for a *gamelan* (traditional percussion orchestra of Southeast Asia). From the decoration surrounding the gamelan, I felt sure that I was in for a treat.

Three rows of ten folding chairs each had been set up for the audience. I also noticed that half way between the front row of these chairs and the stage sat a lone, overstuffed chair. I was ushered to that chair.

Before long, groups of Burmese people gathered, mostly in modified Burmese dress. Some of the men wore characteristically ill-fitting western pants and white shirts, but most were in longyi. The women wore beautiful batik material. Like always in Southeast Asia, the audience sat quietly and attentively. The gamelan, richly dressed in court-type Burmese regalia, entered from a side door to soft applause.

Without warning, the house lights were extinguished and the make-shift theatrical lights lit the stage and the performance began. Some of the dances were country dances, and for these, the costumes were obviously the dress of peasants. Some of the dances, court dances, were highly stylized and dazzling, with tight-fitting, heavily embroidered brocades and glittering crowns. Before each dance, there was a brief explanation in Burmese. The audience was largely silent, except for some gentle applause at the end of each dance, although a little muffled laughter accompanied any comical dance.

The performance continued for about an hour with a short

intermission through which the audience remained seated. At the end, the man who had shown me to my privileged seat came over and asked, "Did you enjoy the performance?" I responded enthusiastically. He said the dancers would like to meet me. When I nodded, the entire troupe of about twenty-five young people in their wonderful costumes and full makeup filed by me. The girls bowed slightly and clasped their hands together beneath their chins; the boys offered vigorous, awkward western handshakes.

The man then introduced me to the troupe leader, an older woman who spoke no English. From his translation, I learned that the dancers were in a school devoted to perpetuating the customs of Myanmar. I thanked the woman profusely and turned to the man and asked, "How much do I owe you?" He said, "Nothing. You are our guest." Needless to say, I was deeply moved even though innumerable experiences had shown me the innate dignity of the Burmese people. Many times I wondered how they could live under their oppressive government, subjected daily to outrageous mistreatment, and yet maintain dignity, grace, and kindness.

On my return to the Strand, I met my new friend, the manager. She asked, "Did you enjoy the performance?" I replied enthusiastically, "Yes!" I told her what had happened and that I wanted to give the troupe some money. She replied, "I heard. They would be insulted. They were so pleased that you came. They felt

honored."

The Palio

(2002)

Although to be in Siena, Italy, for the Palio had long been a dream, it seemed unobtainable until 2002 during a serious conversation with Marco, the concierge, at the Villa La Massa near Florence. At that time, we devised a plan for the following year. In reality "devised" is not quite accurate. Closer to the fact was that Marco said, "I think it can be arranged. I have a cousin."

The best word to describe the Palio is impossible--not unbelievable, but impossible. It occurs each July and August, and although its origins are earlier, the present form evolved during that glorious period, the Renaissance, when humankind's imagination soared. To call the Palio a horse race misses all sense of its being a beautiful, historical, religious, exciting, flamboyant, and thoroughly Italian festival. The Palio is named for the tall vertical banner, richly decorated with the image of the Madonna, the *palio,* that is awarded the winner of the horse race that concludes the festival.

The following year when I arrived at La Massa, Marco told me that he had arranged for my long-dreamed-of visit. He wisely advised that I hire a car to navigate the traffic and crowds. That evening, I was approached by a young English couple, who having heard about my arrangements excitedly asked if they might join me. Even though they did not have the precious tickets for seats, they were willing to take their chances. I welcomed their charming company and the opportunity to share some of the expense of this caper.

Early in the morning, we met Richardo, the driver arranged by Marco. It was a gloriously beautiful day, and we easily arrived in Siena early. It seemed unusual, but I did not question as Richardo drove directly to the center of town and deposited us in a small square to the rear of the duomo. Richardo explained that we should rendez-vous in this square precisely 45 minutes after the race finished.

We had ample time for a pleasant lunch, and by the time we finished, the streets of this medieval city were tightly crowded with excited festival-goers. My new friends and I realized that we had to go our separate ways until after the race. I wished them much luck in finding their way into the beautiful scalloped-shaped central square, the Piazza del Campo, where the main events take place. We bid each other *arrivederci* but viewing the crowds, I literally wondered if we would ever see each other again.

The festival is based on the ancient *contrade* (the official neighborhoods of the city), seventeen in all. One can be a member of a *contrada* only by being born in that neighborhood. There are all sorts of devices to ensure that one is of a certain contrada, but if a man marries a woman from a different contrada, she and he forever remain in different contrade. Were the woman to give birth to a baby while living in yet another neighborhood, they would be a three-contrade family. Each contrada has many local celebrations and events preceding and following the race. Although it is difficult to gain access to these events, there is more than enough to see in all the narrow streets surrounding the Piazza del Campo.

Each contrada has an emblem, the goose, the double-headed eagle, the porcupine, the unicorn, and the like, and each has its own marvelous combination of brilliant colors. Quickly, I yearned to be in a contrada and be allowed to wear loosely tied around my neck one of the colorful emblematic scarves. No one checked any credentials when I purchased my beautiful gold, blue, brown, and black double-headed eagle scarf from a street vendor. Thus, I became a full-fledged member of the *Aquila* (Eagle) contrada for the day.

By early afternoon, the formal contrade processions began to make their way through the maze of streets and throngs of people. Everywhere flags were flying. Banners of red and gold hung from all the balconies. The central part of the city became a brilliant whirl of sounds and colors, a true color-filled cacophony. It was hard to believe that medieval Siena with its narrow streets, thankfully free of cars, could accommodate the crowds and the excitement.

The tension mounted from all quarters of the city as the pounding cadences from the deep drums that preceded each contrada heralded its convergence toward the central piazza. In each group, the drummers were followed by the flag bearers who twirled huge flags depicting the contrada emblem and colors. The marchers were all young men dressed in Renaissance attire with multicolored hose, short velvet jerkins that were richly embroidered and brocaded with gold and jewels, and short capes. Their hats were pork-pie affairs, plumed bonnets, turbans, or simple skull caps. They wore wigs if their hair were not naturally Renaissance length. Strikingly, the young men displayed a genuine seriousness. They showed that they felt they had been selected for something important. The effect was increased by the fact that the faces of these young men are those that decorate the frescoed walls of the palaces of Florence and Siena. (Other than as spectators, there is no role for young women in the Palio).

While proceeding through the narrow streets, at intervals, the processions stopped and the drums increased the cadence as the flag twirlers performed a variety of maneuvers that climaxed in throwing the furled flags high into the air. As the flags descended, they unfurled in a blaze of color and were caught in a continuous twirling.

Following the flags were armored knights on horseback, their horses fully armored or caparisoned with velvet drapery. For the lucky seven contrade that had won the lottery that meant that they would be racing that day, their race horse and jockey followed. These high-spirited animals danced in circles around their groomsmen as they paraded through the streets. The costumed group representing the contrada was followed by young men and women who were themselves colorfully dressed in tight jeans and T-shirts and sang rally songs in a husky unison.

The processions, the throngs of festival-goers, and I all poured into the Piazza del Campo, which had been prepared for the festival. Spectators already packed the balconies, from which hung long red and gold and black and white banners.

Lining the perimeter of the piazza were steep bleachers that bordered the narrow race track. The track itself had been filled in with soil to be somewhat level. Behind a small railing, the large, circular center of the piazza was jam-packed with standing spectators all waving their contrada scarves. Any who fainted in that throng literally fainted vertically and had to be passed hand or over hand over the heads of the crowd to waiting first-aid workers. I later learned that my English friends had found a spot in this morass of humanity and that they were able to watch most of the activity. As for me, through one of his ubiquitous cousins, the magician Marco had arranged a perfect seat. I sat excitedly and relatively comfortably in the shade on the lowest tier of the bleachers near the starting and the finishing line.

At 5:00 p.m. sharp, I heard a cannon fire and the giant bell of the main tower of the city hall began a constant clanging. I am sure that this must be the only event in all of Italy that starts on time. From the side, a squad of mounted carabinieri entered in their blue and red nineteenth-century uniforms, complete with Napoleonic hats. With ceremony they paraded around the race track, suddenly springing into a full charge with their sabers thrust forward. Looking like a Gericault painting, they became a blur of red and blue with flashing steel, hooves, and flying dirt.

Following this thunderous excitement, twelve deep drummers, eighteen trumpeters whose long silver trumpets were festooned with colorful banners, and thirty musicians began a series of fanfares announcing each contrada as it solemnly entered and marched around the ring. At intervals, the deep drums changed their beat and the group, ablaze with emblematic colors, stopped while the flag bearers tossed their twirling flags. Gradually the entire perimeter of the piazza was filled by the marching contrade with flags being tossed high and unfurling in descent. It was one of the most beautiful and colorful sights that I have ever beheld.

Following the contrade came a group of knights in armor with shut visors riding armored horses, each escorted by a squire. Atop each knight's helmet was a symbol of an animal, perhaps 1 foot high, representing a contrada that no longer exists.

Although the procession continued for over 2 hours, there was no flagging of excitement. In fact, the crowd reached a near frenzy when into the piazza arrived a huge war chariot drawn by four giant white oxen each accompanied by an attendant. Riding on the chariot were six long trumpeters playing fanfares on silver trumpets and "nobles" dressed in flowing velvet robes. On the chariot was the precious palio. The beauty of the oxen-pulled cart was exceeded only by one's wonderment as to how it made it through the streets.

A cannon fired to signal that the race was about to begin. The seven lucky spirited horses with their colorful jockeys came to the starting line. I joined the crowd in a crazed massive cheering and scarf-waving.

A gun was fired, and the horses were off. The crowd moaned loudly as the horses were recalled and relined. Again the gun fired, and again the crowd moaned. On the third attempt--for the life of me I could see no difference among the various starts--the seven horses raced around the track three times.

Although lasting only a few minutes, the race is pandemonium. The horses and riders frequently crashed into the walls, sometimes they crashed into the spectators who had jumped over the barriers, and frequently they crashed into each other. The jockeys whipped their horses as well as each other. It is said that there is a strict rule against whipping another's horse. That seemed to be the only restraint that I could detect.

By the end of the third lap, the finish line was completely obscured by the overflow crowds and the police trying to restrain them. The race ended in the midst of this lovely Italian confusion. Without protest, the *Istrice* (Porcupine) was declared the winner. Even though I was seated on the finish line, I have no idea how that was decided.

At this point, all barriers came down, and the people from the bleachers crushed into the center crowd. Everywhere there was wailing, chest pounding, and tears, as well as kisses, embraces, and men being hoisted onto each others' shoulders as the crowd surged toward the palio high above the judges. The surge became a mass of color, singing, cheering, and bemoaning as the throng with the prized banner moved toward the duomo to watch the winning horse and rider be led as conquering heroes up to the high altar. I did not see this ceremony.

Having had more than enough excitement for one day, my thoughts turned to how I would find Richardo and my English friends at our meeting point in the little piazza behind the duomo. I was more than ready to return to my villa in Florence.

As I literally forced my way toward the duomo, it seemed impossible that Richardo would be able to find us, let alone meet us with the car. I began to wonder how it was possible that we had arrived at that piazza in the first place, passing through barricade after barricade with only a wave or a short conversation with the guards.

Despite the seemingly impenetrable crowd, I eventually arrived at the meeting place where my day's adventure began. I spotted Richardo and before long the English couple. Gratefully we all sought refuge in the car, and Richardo, through insistent driving, but without touching his horn, made his way through the crowd. Once again the barricades opened like by magic.

Finally, I could stand it no longer. "Richardo," I asked, "How is it possible that you were able to leave us and pick us up in the center of the town?" With a sly smile, he said, "My cousin is the chief of police."

The Giant Buddha at Nara

(2003)

Probably the title of this book should include the word

"nostalgia," for many of the stories are deeply nostalgic--often for

places visited but once. During the less than an hour train ride from

Kyoto, Japan, to Nara, I was flooded with memories from almost

50 years ago. In my then amateurish explorations of Japan, Nara,

its eighth-century capital, all these years has remained in my mind's

eye with Technicolor vividness. Easily I could picture the great

sacred park with soft light coming through the trees, freely roaming

deer, and the giant Buddha. Nara was first time I had ever been in a

sanctuary.

As the conductor called out, "Nara! Nara!" I was pulled from

my reveries. I had a list of important sites that I wanted to see during

the day's visit. In a conscious attempt not to retrace my steps of long

ago, I planned to visit the Buddha last. My unconscious was to have

it different.

Following a primitive tourist map, I was soon lost. Deep in

the beauty of Nara's famous deer park, I found myself turning right and left. Without realizing it, suddenly I was before the great eighth-century, Tang-style dark brown and white Todaiji Diabutsu-den that houses *Diabutsu* (Buddha). My memory of the shrine was precise including the huge eighth-century bronze octagonal lantern at the entrance.

I mounted the stone steps and entered the great hall with its enormous light pink and rose red wooden pillars and oversized green ornamentation. There he was--huge and dark bronze, seated on his lotus throne, his hands indicating loving-kindness. I was transfixed. Over 50 feet high, the Diabutsu was at once a colossus and the Cosmic Buddha. I could not help but wonder if he remembered me.

Gazing up into his face, it seemed that his head almost touched the ceiling of this ancient timbered structure said to be the largest wooden structure in the world. Despite the magnitude of the hall, Diabutsu's hugeness felt out of proportion. As I slowly walked around him, his immensity and my insignificance increased. I felt uneasy. I recalled a similar feeling when I first saw him 50 years ago. Neither then nor now could I push my thoughts further. All I could feel was the uneasiness.

He was hard to leave, but according to my plan fully to see all of Nara, I forced myself to proceed down my list. I wanted to locate sites that I had not known even existed on my first visit. I wandered through a series of beautiful temples and several pagodas, however my thoughts stayed with the immensity of the Diabutsu and the huge building barely containing his gigantic image. Before long, I was again lost.

Eventually I made my way out of the park. I found a bus stop and mounted a bus that I hoped would take me at least in the direction of the railroad station. Hanging onto the strap next to me was a man in his early thirties, dressed in smart western style. His English was almost without accent. I mentioned that I was revisiting Japan. He was too young to remember World War II or the U.S. occupation, but he was clearly moved by my interest in his country. He said something that harkened to my past. Like an avatar of the unknown man in Nagasaki, he said, "Would you like to see old Japan?"

He told me about a small temple on the very bus line on which we were riding. He explained that he and his family regularly visited the temple. "I think you would enjoy it," he said and apologized, "Unfortunately, I have an important appointment or I would accompany you." Quickly he drew a small map. A few stops later he bowed and said *"Sayonara."*

I left the bus at the stop the young man had designated and found myself in a not-very-distinctive part of Nara. Using the map he drew, I came upon a dirt road and continued on it until I came to a *torii* gate and the temple.

The temple was Tang in style, vermillion in color, and of small scale. It easily could date from the eighth century. As I passed under the torii gate, I felt the familiar quietness of a Shinto shrine. I felt again young and on a quest. I had re-captured a feeling from long ago, the feeling of being in Japan for the first time.

Walking around the temple I found a path leading into a very old and very dense black bamboo forest. Some of the canes were over a foot in diameter. Crossing a small stream on carefully placed rocks, I came to a larger stream and a bamboo bridge. In the distance, perched by a pond, nestled in the giant bamboos, was a small tea house.

I entered. A young woman in kimono assisted me as I removed my shoes, and she silently preceded me down a wooden corridor. She opened a *shoji* screen, bowed, and bid me enter a *tatami* room. Moving to the far wall, she parted another shoji to reveal the pond and the forest. Silently she disappeared.

Soon I heard a slight shuffle, and without a spoken word the woman reentered the room, bringing tea and small savories. In typical Japanese style, she sat on her heels, back erect, while she poured the tea. She then rose and bowed. As she slid back a shoji to leave, she turned to face me and bowed once again. I was ecstatic to find this idyllic place and to be there alone.

My thoughts kept returning to the giant Buddha and the sense of disproportion that I had felt by his towering in the hall. Could it be that he simply was too large for his surroundings? I had read that the hall had required several rebuildings over the centuries. Perhaps it had been restored to bad proportions.

Years of studying great art from a psychoanalytic perspective have led me to be suspicious of practical explanations for what sometimes seem to be errors, inconsistencies, or ambiguities. Like in the dream, I have found that in great art that which were regarded as errors, inconsistencies, or ambiguities often hide latent condensed meanings that, when unpacked, enrich the understanding. As Stephen Dedalus says in James Joyce's *Ulysses,* "A man of genius makes no mistakes. His errors are volitional and are the portals of discovery." As a psychoanalyst, I might have a different idea regarding "volitional" in the creative but "portals of discovery" perfectly describes my view.

I forced myself to think about the uneasiness I felt in the Buddha's presence and had a half-thought remembering a similar feeling when I was in Bangkok, Thailand, and saw the giant sleeping golden Buddha at Wat Po. The way I felt as I looked up at the face of the giant Buddha of Nara was similar to the way I felt as I walked along the great length of the Thai Buddha. With both, I sensed the immensity and my insignificance.

Suddenly it became clear. Standing before the giant Buddha re-creates the feeling of being the small child looking up at the mother. Being next to the sleeping giant re-creates the feeling of the small child being along side the mother's sleeping body. I had the delicious feeling of a psychoanalytic epiphany. Once again psychoanalytic awareness of atavistic and anachronistic experience enriched my understanding of art and religion and brought the two into close alignment.

A Messenger from Above

(2003)

I must admit that I reluctantly planned my return trip to
Japan. After 50 years, I feared that although this beautiful and exotic
Asian country was important to me during my formative years, that
now it and I would be too changed. I remembered while in the U.S.
Navy on the *USS Prairie* in the Inland Sea seeing a gigantic, vivid
vermillion *torii* gate rising out of the water. I later learned that the
gate was part of a temple on a sacred island rarely visited. For my
return to Japan, I was determined to visit that island, Miyajima,
hoping to recapture the experience of discovering Japan. I was not to
be disappointed.

I was delighted to learn that the island remained little
developed other than the temple complex, a few small *ryokans* (inns),
and some shops. I was told that although historically there were
many restrictions as to who could visit the island, these were no
longer enforced and the island now was heavily visited. I was also
assured that except for the few visitors at the ryokans, the island
emptied at night.

Near Hiroshima, Miyajima was a 10-minute ferry ride off the mainland in the Seto Inland Sea. Those brief minutes transport one into another realm, a spiritual realm that inhabits a tiny rocky island marked by deep coves of intensely blue water and a center peak, Misen San, rising nearly 1,800 feet. My autumnal visit allowed me to glory in the deep green pines, brilliantly red maples, and beautiful yellow ginkgoes.

I enthusiastically hiked the many secluded trails from the sea to the mountain top. Near the sea, munching on ginkgoes in the grass-covered meadows were thousands of sacred deer, *shinroku* (messengers from the gods). These freely roaming deer scarcely took notice as I walked by. Also not the least bit shy, in the high reaches of the island I saw many chattering monkeys, ever ready to rob the unwary of sunglasses, cameras, or hiking bags, especially if they contained food.

The four-legged vermillion torri gate whose image I had carried for 50 years was set in a deep inlet and towered over 50 feet high. It was part of Itsukushima, a famous Shinto shrine, set in a place of changing moods. During high water, the gate seemed to float away into the misty sea and the entire temple appeared afloat. When the tide was out, I could walk to the gate on the firm mud flats and look back at the temple helplessly stranded on pilings.

Happily I spent several magical days in the over-150-years-old Iwaso Ryokan that sat on a small hill overlooking the blessed cove. Adding endless charm, my *tatami* room opened onto a running brook and a small forest. The ryokan was the perfect place for me.

Increasingly wishing I would never leave this paradise, on the jetty I found a favorite viewing place for the gate, the shrine, and a lovely five-tiered pagoda on a hill nearby. Faithfully, I returned many times to my special spot to imbibe the variations in tidal patterns and the changing light. How fortunate I was to be able to see the shrine during high tide, low tide, in the moonlight, at dawn, and at sunset.

On my last evening, I seated myself to watch the setting sun heighten the bright red of the shrine and the gate. As the rising moon cast a long path to the entrance of the shrine and the small nearby village gently lighted its *shojis,* I was transfixed with wonder. I stared in awe at the scene before me--until I felt a tugging at my hip pocket.

I was outraged as I thought that someone was pick-pocketing me. Suddenly I became deeply forlorn. "How can anyone ruin my bliss," I thought. Instinctively I called out, "Son of a bitch!" and quickly slapped my hand over my back pocket. To my astonishment, I discovered that a deer had poked his sacred nuzzle into my pocket and was pleasantly munching away on my return railroad ticket.

Unconcerned, he slowly walked away, my ticket in his mouth. I ran after him, attempting to snatch it back. All I could think was that indeed he was a messenger from above doing the bidding of the gods. They wanted me to stay, as my Western conscience fought saying it was time for me to move on.

Bali and Java

(2005)

Scuba

I have always thought of Bali as paradise on earth, and I knew
that someday I would visit. Despite the horrific terrorist bombings
on October 12, 2002, at Bali's Jimbaran Beach, I forged ahead with
my plans. I was sure that the attack was an aberration. Little did I
know that I would be visiting Bali and Java between bombings, for on
October 1, 2005, a month after my visit, there was a second terrible
bombing and not too long thereafter a devastating earthquake.

Generally, I am not interested in the pleasures and activities
that places like Jimbaran offer, but I had a secret goal. Over the years
and in several countries, I had tried to arrange a scuba experience.
Each time, I must admit sometimes to my relief, something came up
that made it impossible. Despite and probably because of my age,
this time I was determined to succeed, and the visit to Bali seemed
the perfect opportunity.

The plan was clear. The beach days would be devoted to
scuba, and then I would go inland to Ubud to explore extensively the

sacred and artistic sights of the island's interior.

Wary of the scuba adventure, I thought I had better make arrangements at the "high end." I booked at the Four Seasons Hotel at Sayan on Jimbaran Bay and asked the hotel to arrange for the scuba. As it turned out, staying at the Four Seasons was propitious. It was easy to arrange to spend a short time at their Jimbaran hotel and the greater part of my stay at their beautiful hotel in Ubud.

After many e-mails with the hotel I was put in touch with Bali International Diving Professionals, whose literature offered "Discover Scuba Diving" as one of the levels of scuba. The description noted that no prior experience was necessary and that little time need be spent in instruction. I said to myself, "Perfect."

As I settled into my beautiful villa on the water's edge with a full view of Jimbaran Bay and the surrounding lush mountains, I received a note from Bali International Diving Professionals saying that I would be picked up at 6:00 a.m. the next morning. Again, perfect.

After an early and hearty breakfast of special eggs (the chef took seriously my casual comment about an interest in different kinds of eggs: one day, goose; the second, quail; the third, duck), I was met by Ali and Mohammed, two rather sullen-faced boys in a beat-up van. I confess to having felt somewhat disconcerted, but I decided to forge ahead regardless.

Mohammed handed me a large book of illustrations and explanations, and he suggested that I read it while we drove. The book contained the basics of scuba, and Mohammed added further information and directions. His efficient and yet gentle way gave me renewed confidence in the undertaking.

I had not expected an hour-long ride, but I was not sorry because I saw beautiful Bali awakening as we drove over back roads and through villages. Often I was offered processions of gorgeous Balinese women in sarongs carrying a variety of objects on their heads and an occasional temple procession with garlanded participants, gongs, and drums.

Eventually we arrived at a shack with a weathered sign on which was written "Bali International Diving Professionals." Underneath was scribbled "The Dive Shop." My confidence lessened. It sunk to a new low as we tried on wet suit after wet suit. Obvious scuba is a sport for the young and the thin, especially in Bali. With great patience, Mohammed and Ali eventually found a suit that I could stuff myself into by removing my bathing suit and wearing only Jockeys. We then drove another hour to the beach. I realized that although I had chosen the right hotel for comfort and luxury, it was a long way from the diving areas. By the time we arrived at the diving destination, Tulamban Beach, we had crossed over one-third of the island.

Already on the beach were several other beat-up old vans and cars. In comparison, my beat-up old van was in excellent condition. Mohammed and Ali began unloading and checking the equipment. I could not help but notice the procession of old and young Balinese women carrying tanks and various pieces of diving equipment on their heads to and from the beach. Ali told me this was the local custom. I learned later that the dive companies were required to hire women to carry the equipment and the women do it according to local custom, on their heads.

Tulamban is on a wide bay on the Northeastern coast of the Sea of Bali. For Bali, it is not beautiful, but the surf is gentle. The van crossed the grass to the edge of the pebbly beach.

It took both Mohammed and Ali to sausage me into the wet suit and fit the long fins. Mohammed checked the dive mask with corrected lenses that I had brought from the United States and said, "Great!" He motioned for me to move toward the water's edge. The gentle surf lapped around my ankles. Skillfully the two boys adjusted a weight belt around my waist and placed tanks on my back. I needed a lot of help to move. I felt and looked like a 747 lumbering down the runway. Mohammed said a short prayer as we entered the water. I was glad that he was Muslim and not Hindu. I do not think I could have stood long enough for propitiation to a multitude of gods.

When I was about waist-deep in the water I thought, "What on Earth am I doing going into the water with heavy weights around my waist and heavy tanks on my back?" To my great relief, Mohammed suggested that I squat in the water up to my neck. Suddenly the 747 was airborne. I felt light and able as the warm Sea of Bali gave me flotation.

Mohammed stayed with me, and Ali returned to the beach. I followed Mohammed's instructions closely and began to feel some mastery of the situation. He explained and demonstrated the necessary breathing technique, taught me how to free my mask of water, and instructed me in the simple hand signals by which we could communicate under water. He explained that he would control my depth and that he would be at my side at all times. He added, "Ali is on the beach, always watching us in case of a difficulty." We then tried complete submersion with my feet firmly on the rocky bottom. After about ten practice submersions, Mohammed said, "Splendid," and he indicated that I should follow him. I am a strong swimmer but could only barely keep up with him.

We swam on the surface about 500 yards out into the sea

and approached a reef. As the water began to churn near the reef, Mohammed helped me adjust my breathing apparatus and together we descended. I went up and down the face of the reef. I have never felt more ecstatic nor seen anything more beautiful. I have snorkeled all over the world, but in those 30 minutes the variety and beauty of what I saw far exceeded anything before. I have never felt that kind of exaltation.

All too soon Mohammed indicated that we should go to the surface. I sadly did what I was told, fearing that my "Discover Scuba Diving" experience was over. We rose to the surface, and with a broad smile Mohammed said, "You are now ready for a dive!" He began swimming north and west with me in gleeful pursuit.

At a point he said, "Let's dive!" and began adjusting my equipment. We descended into the bluish grey water lighted by streaks of sunlight from above. Gradually, I made out lurking on the bottom the sunken frame of the *USS Liberty*, a small U.S. Navy cargo vessel that had been torpedoed during World War II. I felt a curious affinity in that I remembered that the Liberty-class ships had been hurriedly assembled in makeshift shipyards in Sausalito, California (my home of the last 45 years), during the war.

Together Mohammed and I explored the vessel. A wide array of fish swam peacefully among brightly colored coral growths on the skeletal remains of the ship. I watched as they eerily darted by a search light and a piece of the bridge and swam in lazy formations among the huge blades of the screws. At one point, I looked up and saw a fellow diver. His rhythmic movements added to my feeling that I had joined a world that I would never forget, a beautiful world silent save for the hypnotic cadence of my breathing, its bubbles forcing their way about my head to the surface. I was thrilled beyond explanation.

I had lost all sense of time and direction when Mohammed tapped my shoulder to show me that my air gauge needle bordered on red. With his thumb he indicated that we must surface. As he adjusted a dial, reluctantly I began to move upward. I was powerless to remain in my newfound world. I was like a baby being forced from his mother's womb.

We swam back to the beach, and with Ali's help I was relieved of the fins, belt, and tanks. The boys showed me how to unzip my suit and pull it down to my waist. Following Mohammed, I went to a shack on the beach for a late lunch. We joined several other divers, young Australians, all with their suits unzipped and pulled down to their waists. I felt young and a part of an exclusive fraternity. Their talk, like that of aviators, was rarely of what they had seen but how deep they had gone and how they had managed one difficult situation after another. They were exchanging "war stories." One asked me how deep I had gone, and Mohammed said about 55 feet. The young man kindly said, "That is the perfect depth for maximum light and color." I felt very pleased.

As we drove back, Mohammed asked me how old I was. I replied, "Seventy-seven." After a pause, he said, "You are the oldest person I have ever taught to dive." After was a silence, he added, "You are the oldest person I have ever talked to."

When I returned to the hotel, I could not find enough people to tell about my experience, a problem that has continued to this day. I sent an e-mail to my attorney, "Sell everything. I am going to open a dive shop in Bali." His response, "Be sure you have a spare room for me."

Bali

Hindu Bali is an island of endless beauty and interest. The temples, never tall, emerge from the jungle as a series of portals, pavilions, and grotesque images, roughly carved in hard, sharp-edged, dark red, almost black volcanic stone. One evening I visited the sixteenth-century Hindu temple, Pura Tanah Lot, perched on a cliff above the Indian Ocean, to witness a performance of the *Ramayana*. The setting sun set the temple ablaze and frosted pink the waves crashing below. The *Ramayana* spectacle was mesmerizing. I watched by bonfire light as a chorus of over fifty half-naked men in white loin cloths in crescendos of *kecak* clucking with stretched out arms and fingers surrounded and musically accented the heavily costumed and stylized principals who acted out the drama through dance.

In inland Bali, with a guide, I descended the narrow road leading to Pura Tirta Empul, a tenth-century temple nestled in a thickly vegetated ravine. Tumbling down the mountainside, the temple marked the emergence of the Pakrisan River from its high mountain origins with a series of carved rock terraces and park-like green and flowered expanses. At the lowest level, the temple expanded into a series of rectangular rock pools that was fed by a line of carved phantasmagoric heads spouting cool water.

It was by good fortune that we had it all to ourselves. I could not resist asking my guide if I might bathe in one of the pools. He seemed hesitant. I am sure it was because I am not Hindu and therefore, like anyone who eats meat and wears leather, I was contaminated. However, with a smile he said, "Quickly, before anyone comes." In moments I was splashing in the freshness of the water. Suddenly a Hindu priest appeared at the pool's edge. I feared I was in trouble. He smiled, gave a characteristic greeting, and silently proceeded with his ablution.

Ubud

I was strolling late one evening after visiting the many wood carving shops and artisan studios in and around Ubud, never tiring of examining the intricacy and detail in these world-renown wood carvings. As an aside, I did not realize that besides being a bush, hibiscus is also a kind of tree. Carvings made from hibiscus have an extraordinarily rich chocolate-colored swirling grain that alternates suddenly with narrow strips of lemon yellow. Even though I had taken a vow of abstinence with regard to buying yet more objects, I broke my vow. I could not resist buying a dancer carved from this extraordinary wood.

I am neither sure of the location nor how I got there, but walking down an alley, somewhat lost, I was sure I heard a *gamelan* (percussion orchestra of Indonesia) coming from what seemed a shabby hut. I poked my head inside and saw about twenty rusted folding chairs arranged on the dirt floor under a bare electric light bulb hanging from the roof. In front of the chairs was a large white sheet held up at the corners by clothes pins. A young Belgian backpacker was seated, and a few young Balinese men were lounging about. I asked the Belgian if she knew what was going on. She said that she had heard that in a half hour there would be a puppet show.

Soon more Balinese gathered, the light was turned off, and

the gamelan began. There was the characteristic screeching and aphonic crying of the cantor. Suddenly a huge torch was lighted behind the sheet. The shadow of its flickering was itself magical. Equally suddenly the shadows of the puppets appeared on the sheet. For the next 90 minutes I and my fellow traveler sat transfixed as much by the ever-changing flickering of the torch as by the shadows of the puppets performing the *Ramayana*. I had stumbled upon an authentic Balinese puppet show set up for the sole pleasure of the neighborhood.

The show ended with much applause from the appreciative audience. I suggested to my Belgian friend that we see what was behind the screen. There, below a rough platform, was a complete gamelan with twelve young musicians. On the platform were several older puppeteers carefully putting their leather prizes into long boxes. Behind them was the torch, a large metal cone filled with coconut straw and fueled by kerosene. We talked with the musicians and the puppeteers. They were delighted by our interest and amid much laughter they demonstrated their instruments and let us clumsily manipulate the puppets.

Java

Java is not as beautiful as Bali. The beaches are not as white and the shoreline not as craggy, but Java has an unspoiled quality that Bali has lost. The population, largely Muslim, does not have the colorfulness of Bali's Hindus. Yet however strained our relation with the Muslim world unfortunately has become, I felt warmly welcomed. I must say that I never tire of hearing the *muezzin* call to prayer, especially before dawn. Never can I hear that plaintive wail without my memory returning to a visit to a tiny remote *kasbah* reached only by mule high above Marrakech in the lower Moroccan Atlas Mountains. The kasbah, alone on a mountain peak with the majestic snow-covered mountains behind, overlooked a misty deep red valley below. Beautiful, clear, and echoing from mountain to mountain from an invisible mosque somewhere in the mist came the call to prayer, sweet and pure. What a treat it was for it was without electronic amplification.

Although I have a special fondness for Hindu temples, even though the the ninth-century Candi Prambanan in Java is one of the most beautiful Hindu complexes that can be visited, it was my exploration of the austere grandeur of the eighth-century Buddhist Borobudur that brought the greatest satisfaction from my visit to Indonesia. A gigantic step-pyramid with many tiers holding deeply carved bas-reliefs relating the life of the Buddha, Borobudur was rewarding at dawn, midday, evening, and by moonlight. Taken together, the volcanic blocks become a gigantic monolithic mandala. As one ascends into the metaphoric enlightenment of the cosmic Mount Meru, the stupas on the highest level, free of human representations, are a lattice of simple squares and diamonds. The squares with their flat undersurface reinforce a sense of stability; the diamonds perched on end, develop a sense of dynamic tension.

Happily, I chose to stay at the Amanjiwo Hotel. Designed to be an abstracted version of Borobudur, the Amanjiwo is a series of beautiful pavilions and villas. By good fortune my villa commanded a view of the great temple in the distance.

The hotel was rather empty, and there were few English-speaking guests. I quickly made friends with the managers, Australian Sean Flakelar and his lovely English wife Lindsay, who seemed happy to have English-speaking company. In any case, rarely did I have dinner without one or the other joining me, reviewing my adventures, and helping plan my next day.

At one such dinner, a dinner prepared for me by Sean himself, the suggestion was made that I could best visit a particular temple by elephant. How appealing! It was arranged that I would meet the elephant the next morning.

I asked about a guide, and Sean explained that one was unnecessary because the elephant came with a mahout who knew the way. I was interested to learn that the elephants in Java all come from

Sumatra and that the mahouts come with them.

Much has been written about the mystical link between the elephant and humankind often related to the fact that the Old Testament gives human life 82 years, approximately the same natural life span as the elephant. I was fascinated to learn that in Sumatra when the elephants are about age 7, they are linked with a boy of the same age who becomes his lifetime caretaker and companion.

Early the next morning at the arranged spot I heard the clump, clump, clump of a huge beast. I was startled to see two elephants emerge from the jungle. I greeted the mahout and said, "There must be some mistake. I am alone. I really need only one elephant." The young boy grinned and said with much diffidence, "Don't worry, professor. We only charge you for one elephant. You see, this one is the sweetheart of this one," pointing to the elephant mounted with the *howdah*. "He won't go anywhere without her."

Like a procession, we advanced through the jungle, crossing streams, and passing though small villages where children came running out to see and feed the great beasts. The temple was a bit of a disappointment, however I enjoyed every minute of the adventure as my elephant dutifully followed his love. I might add, though, that riding 3 hours in a howdah is a little like being in a very long earthquake.

A Princely Wedding in Delhi

(2008)

As I was enjoying the pool at the Shangri-La Hotel in
Bangkok, Thailand, recovering from the 18 hours of flying from San
Francisco on my way to Delhi, India, I hardly could believe that
all had come together seamlessly. Months before while planning a
trip to the Himalayan plateau including Bhutan, Northern Burma
(Myanmar), Yunnan Province, and Lhasa, I e-mailed my plans to my
friend, Katie Bhathena, a lovely Parsi woman in Bombay, to see if
we could meet. Although it would have been easier to go to Delhi, I
offered to come to Bombay. To my astonishment she responded, "No
need to come to Bombay, I will be in Delhi. At that very time I will
be attending a princely wedding and if you come we can go together."

It had been some time since I last visited India, and I
knew that much had happened to the Bhathena family. Our first
meeting was many years ago when Katie attended a conference in
San Francisco. Evie and I had offered to be the "hosts" for another
attendee, a lovely Norwegian woman, who had quickly made friends
with Katie. Katie was unhappily placed and began spending time

with our guest and with us. Quickly we became friends, never imagining that she and her family would several times be our gracious hosts on visits to India.

The Parsi community is unique in India. They are Persians who migrated South in the seventh century when the Muslims invaded Iran and attempted forcefully to convert the Iranians from Zoroastrianism to Islam. Holding strongly to their Zoroastrian religion, the largest community settled in Bombay. Because of their language, an early form of Farsi, they became known as Parsi. Always a tightly closed community, they established Zoroastrian fire temples, maintained their religious practices, and very much discouraged intermarriage with Indians. From early on they were renown for ingenuity, entrepreneurship, industriousness, and social programs for their community. With my interest in religious practice, I eagerly looked forward to some day visiting with the Bhathenas in India and learning more about their remarkably early form of monotheism and abstraction of providential forces, ritual fire worship, and unique manner of dealing with death.

Some day arrived in 1978, when Evie and I made our first visit to India. We of course contacted Katie in Bombay to tell her of our plans. When we landed in Delhi, we were astonished to be met at the airport by two young, handsomely dressed Indian men with a luxurious Mercedes. "We are from the Bhathena Company and were sent by the Bhathena family to meet you and to assure your comfort and enjoyment during your visit to India," said one in a clipped British accent. It never occurred to us that Katie's family might be extraordinarily influential, wealthy, and would provide us with guardianship and caring assistance at nearly every site we visited during our explorations of India.

Since that wonder-filled trip, Evie and I were saddened to learn that Katie and her husband, Darius, had divorced. However the friendship with Katie continued, refreshed by her several visits to San Francisco. Always a strongly independent woman, Evie and I enjoyed hearing about the events in Katie's family and in India. We were especially amazed to learn that Katie had taken up racecar driving and had become, to quote the *Hindu Times*, " . . . the fastest woman in India."

As unbelievable as this was, I recently learned that her daughter, Navaz, whom I remember as a little girl, astonishingly enough had also become a prize-winning racecar driver, "the Queen of the Tarmac," as the *Hindu Times* proclaimed. Adding to the excitement, Navaz had married a young Sikh, Karandip Sandhu, a fellow prize-winning racecar driver. I also learned that Karandip was the scion of an aristocratic noble family of the Punjab.

In our e-mails to plan my 2008 visit, Katie enticingly added that if I spent more time in India, after the wedding we could go with Navaz and Karandip to visit some of Karandip's palaces and forts in the Punjab, as well as the Golden Temple at Amristar, where Karandip's ancestors were honored as part of the founding aristocratic martyrs of the Sikh religion. It was all too much to resist.

The Princely Wedding

The 1,500 gold-embossed invitations from the Begum Shahradi Abbul Hai were hand addressed and delivered by courier. Each envelope contained requests for attendance at the six separate parties celebrating the wedding of her grandson Zahid to the television star Aashti. Of the events, I was told, the most resplendent would be the wedding ceremony. Karandip and Zahid, the grandson of the Nawab of Palanpur, were best friends and had been school mates in a fashionable private school for Indian aristocrats.

In the best Indian and Sikh tradition, Karandip greeted me upon my arrival as though I were a member of the family, assuring me that even though it was to be an "intimate" wedding, I would be welcome. Indeed, I was.

In that Aashti and Zahid are both Muslims, the events began with the bride and groom being separately attended by their "followers." As part of the groom's party, I went with my friends to the groom's grandmother's palatial home. As we arrived we were greeted by the agonizing moaning of strange voices and drumming. In the corner of the huge living room on a rug were a small collection of ancient cronies and musicians. I was told that they were villagers from the family's ancestral village who came to pay their respects, ward off evil spirits, and assure fecundity.

The room was laced with heavy Victorian furniture and innumerable turn-of-the century pictures and memorabilia identifying the family's noble heritage and visits by and to English aristocracy. Against one wall, the handsome 30-year-old groom was seated on a throne of golden pillows, elegant in his golden brocaded Nehru jacket, white leggings, and jeweled slippers. His uncle, a senior representative of the family, elegantly attired in a multicolored jeweled paisley patterned jacket and turban, was adjusting the groom's golden turban loosely low over one ear in the Rajasthani style. At the proper moment the Begum presented the ancestral turban pin, a ruby-, emerald-, and diamond-encrusted pin with towering egret feathers.

The groom and his party were now ready to proceed to the bride's family villa, an enormous walled garden in the ancient part of Delhi not far from the Qutub Minar. We preceded the groom's car and lined the narrow streets outside the walls of the villa to cheer and applaud as he entered. As the groom's car approached, huge torches were lighted at the entrance of the villa's portcullis, and two giant drums pounded by men in white loin cloths began a slowly increasing beat. The groom leading his party entered the gateway and proceeded joyfully through the thick walls of the villa into the garden. The entire gateway from street into the garden was covered by overhead tenting and wall curtains of white orchids rimmed with red carnations.

The groom's party filed into a portion of the torch-lit garden and was seated on cushions placed among the lush greenery and towers of flowers. An army of red-jacketed and brass-buttoned servants brought trays and trays of food and drinks while musicians strategically seated wailed at their ancient instruments.

The groom, profiled by a giant brass lattice containing about 250 lighted oil lamps, elegantly seated himself on a throne of golden cushions. Each of his well-wishers filed by to pay homage. Suddenly a colorful fire works display filled our sky with giant chrysanthemums and weeping willows and cacophonous drumming signified that the marriage contract had been signed. The groom arose and led the procession of his party through multiple flowered archways into the other part of the garden where the bride and her party waited.

The bride in a gorgeous golden sari and abundant pearls

and jewels waited on a golden throne of cushions, her face partially covered by a jeweled, golden head covering. Her feet and hands were decorated with carefully designed henna arabesques.

The groom took his place beside his bride and gently placed his hand on hers. Tenderly he lifted her veil. Even though the couple had been dating almost a year, with studied carefulness, he looked surprised and pleased at her beauty, a nod to the tradition of arranged marriage of which this one was not. The marriage was now complete, and the well-wishers filed by.

The guests, the aged Nawab, princes and princesses, young and old members of Indian Muslim and Sikh nobility and aristocracy, officers of the armed forces, and many representatives of the modern television industry of India, were, to say the least, gorgeous.

The women in colorful saris proudly wore ancestral jewelry, multitiered necklaces, ropes of pearls, and earrings so heavily laden with rubies, pearls, emeralds, and sapphires that they had to be supported by ties around the tops of the ears. Some of the women wore jeweled partial face coverings. Most of the men were in black, red, or golden Nehru jackets and white leggings. The Sikhs with their carefully tended beards and tightly wrapped turbans of fuchsia, pink, gold, black, and light blue at times seemed like a field of tulips. Every one spoke with modulated Edwardian English accents and most, including the women, had studied abroad in England and the United States.

A vast buffet supper was then served to the over 1,000 guests (an intimate wedding, as mentioned). At 11:30 p.m. guests began to leave so that they could prepare for the next-day reception at the groom's estate. Several lamented that there would not be many more such weddings in Delhi and certainly none more princely.

Choosing not to attend subsequent opulent events given by the groom's family, Katie, Karandip, Navaz, and I left the next day for a never-to-be-forgotten visit to Amristar, the Golden Temple, and Karandip's various palaces, forts, and estates before I journeyed into the Himalayas.

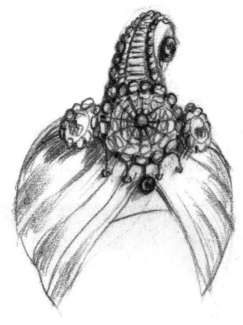

Postscript

In thinking about these memories, it is clear that I have
a fascination with remote and exotic places; places where we feared
eating the food and drinking the water; and places to which I often
had to drag my ever-patient wife, Evie. When asked, I usually
rationalize these compelling pursuits as an intellectual interest in the
relation of art and arcane ritual. At times, I can own up to the fact
that I enjoy playing the role of the overlord in countries that still have
vestiges of colonial traditions, an enjoyment that came from watching
many movies during my youth.

Recently while reading travel guides about Indonesia, I
had one of those psychoanalytic epiphanies regarding many of the
experiences in this book. Despite years of psychoanalysis and years
of the kind of self-analysis that a psychoanalyst does daily, I came to
a new realization. While looking at the lush and colorful pictures
of Bali and Java, in my mind's eye, I revisited myself as a timid boy
growing up in remote, arid Wyoming. I can picture myself eagerly
awaiting the monthly arrival of my cherished *National Geographic*
Magazine. As early as I can remember, I would pour over page after

page. In a dream-like state, I would think myself into far-away places and pursuing exotic activities.

Even though my cunning unconscious long was successful in keeping me from knowing why it had selected and stored only certain places illustrated in the magazine, it was in researching the visit to Indonesia that I clearly realized the startlingly simple fact. The places destined were places that in every way were light years away from the horizonless miles of sagebrush and staid conservatism of southwestern Wyoming. Most of the places I yearned to visit were exotic paradises.

Thinking of my wanderings in that way put a new perspective on a mental practice that had long puzzled me. On a level of half-awareness, I realized that I "ticked off" one at a time the places in the world that I was seeing. I now realize that I was making into reality, one by one, those precious fantasies that allowed me to survive the frequently mind-numbing unhappiness of childhood and adolescence.

My visits in the Middle East--Iran, Jordan, and Egypt--stood out as striking exceptions. Although I have vivid memories from these remarkable places, being there came with a shocking reality. Their terrain looked amazingly like southwestern Wyoming. In fact, in Egypt I remember the uncanny feeling of returning home.

Serendipity

A few of the experiences in this volume are easily recognizable as fortuitous, fortunate, and frequently formative. Many carry the subjective sense of a discovery of things unsought--in short, serendipitous. With notable frequency, the serendipitous experiences involved *a someone* who appeared at a critical moment. Thinking about these incidents aroused my curiosity about serendipity.

In the mid-eighteenth century, Horace Walpole wrote a friend, "I once read a silly fairy tale called *The Three Princes of Serendip*. As their highnesses traveled, they were always making discoveries, by accident and sagacity, of things which they were not in quest of."

Serendip is the old Arabic name for Sri Lanka. Because the three princes were from Serendip and Sri Lanka rightly is associated with the exotic and beautiful, serendipity came to mean making beautiful, wonderful discoveries by accident. Walpole's mention of sagacity, that is, wisdom and the readiness to comprehend, is unfortunately rarely considered part of serendipity.

The adjective serendipitous describes a quality of an event. We say, "The meeting was serendipitous." However, Walpole noted something further. He suggested that the princes in the story repeatedly made wonderful discoveries. When repeatedly is emphasized, the noun *serendipity* becomes the faculty of happening upon fortunate discoveries. Psychoanalytically this suggests that rather than accidental, serendipity involves intrapsychic readiness.

Some Notes on Psychodynamics and Serendipity

Psychoanalyst and child researcher René Spitz noted that children say *no* before they say *yes*. *No* is the word of safety; it closes off possibilities. *Yes* opens possibilities and increases risk. Saying *yes* in personal relationships opens risks of disappointment and rejection. Spitz's observations suggest that the ability to say *yes,* that is, to be inclusive and move into things, comes with maturity and psychic stability. To be more precise, the ability to say *yes* increases as the self becomes more integrated and consolidated and the external world more known and trusted.

Sigmund Freud noted that fate is character. In this simple but profound idea, Freud suggested that often what is ascribed to fate is in fact the unconscious operating in its characteristically unrecognizable way. We unconsciously bring about things that seem to happen to us. William Shakespeare poetically exposed this idea in *Julius Caesar* (Act 1, Scene 2). Cassius says, "The fault, Dear Brutus, is not in our stars / But in ourselves, that we are underlings."

Subsequent psychoanalytic theorists in their study of the development of character described the child's evolution from being a *no* sayer to becoming a *yes* sayer. In effect, the child goes through a series of developmental stages during which conducive and positive experiences with significant people are gradually internalized and integrated. These experiences build up a stable sense of self-integration, self-worth, and trust; and, *pari passu,* there is positive resolution of the major ambivalences that are integral to development.

With self-integration and self-worth, the child emerges as a person who has an inner chorus that reassures and encourages, providing self-assurance and self-confidence even during the most challenging circumstances. The individual says *yes* to an increasing range of opportunities, and life becomes richer.

Conversely, when the significant individuals in one's life have been largely disappointing or the environment has proven untrustworthy, major ambivalences remain unresolved and the individual is filled with self-doubt, self-criticism, distrustfulness, and inhibition. In short, such individuals are fearful of reaching out, of saying *yes*. *No* becomes their ubiquitous response, and their life becomes increasingly circumscribed.

I suggest that an integrated, consolidated, positive sense of self and trust of other allows an individual the confidence and assurance to move into and exploit, in the best sense of that word, new situations. However, self-assurance and self-confidence by themselves do not provide an explanation for the essential quality of serendipity, the subjective sense of "making discoveries, by accident . . . of things . . . not in quest of."

Making Discoveries by Accident of Things . . . Not in Quest Of

It is difficult to explain serendipity without recognizing the dynamic action of the unconscious as it affects our lives. The unconscious is composed of repressed, archaic, infantile drives and early wishes and memories, many of which are maintained with photographic vividness. Optimal mental functioning and stability evidence boundaries and a dynamic equilibrium between the conscious and unconscious psychical systems. With increasing integration and consolidation of the personality, there is lessened fear of being overwhelmed by the unconscious atavistic, anachronistic, archetypical urges, wishes, and memories and a controlled fluidity develops between the systems. This fluidity manifests itself in dreaming, wit, slips of the tongue, and most dramatically as creativity. Essentially it is the interplay between conscious and unconscious processes that enriches and enlivens our everyday mental life.

Inspiration, Epiphany, the Uncanny, and Serendipity

Psychoanalysis calls the controlled fluidity between the unconscious and the conscious *regression in the service of the ego.* Some individuals experience such regression in the service of the ego as moments of inspiration. In past eras, such momentary "visitations" from the unconscious were conceptualized as visits from the muse or revelations from the gods. The individuals whom we call creative are those who are able to take such moments of inspiration and play with and elaborate on them, often in wondrous ways, to bring forth something new. This is the essence of creativity. In fact, the word creativity derives from the Indo-European root *kare* meaning to give birth.

When the thoughts associated with such regressions are elaborate, the thoughts are felt to be epiphanic. Subjectively there is a sense of intuitive perception or insight into an essential meaning that is sometimes initiated by a strikingly simple or ordinary occurrence. Often the feeling of new discovery is mixed with a curious sense of having known it all along and a sense of certainty. Of course, certainty does not equate with truth.

When an event coincides isomorphically with an unconscious fantasy, wish, or memory, the event is experienced as uncanny. The event is remembered with almost visual vividness and is often associated with telepathic or prescient explanation. In fact, early in his exploration of the unconscious, Freud offered this idea as a rational explanation for the uncanny and a large variety of paranormal phenomena.

I suggest that the feeling that an incident is serendipitous is related to inspiration, the epiphany, and the uncanny. I suggest that the sense of serendipity is a momentary ego regression when a person is presented with an opportunity that resonates with an unconscious wish or memory and then *acts* upon it. The opportunity when acted upon sagaciously is subjectively experienced as wondrous and, like Walpole described, "having been come upon."

Applying this idea regarding the psychodynamics of serendipity, the experiences reported in this slender volume that rotate around *an other,* never to be known and never to be forgotten, maintain a vivid profile in my mind. These experiences have become indelibly and with high poignancy a part of me. Around them, I associate strong feelings of having been bettered.

I cannot help but speculate about the unconscious underpinnings of these fully serendipitous meetings. I am tempted to think that those unknown strangers whom I "blindly" followed and to whom I owe much were manifestations of those unconsciously held childhood companions, the various nameless and never to be known authors of the *National Geographic,* who unfailingly proved trustworthy companions during some very dark days.

In reviewing the events reported in this volume, I hope the reader will find all of them interesting, some of them poignant, and a few, humorous. Some, like the feeling of returning home that I had in Egypt, I regard as uncanny, and some like my visit to Sinan's Hammam, may have even been creative. Meeting the man from Nagasaki, however, was pure serendipity.